Dugan's Bistro and the Legend of the Bearded Lady

BY OWEN KEEHNEN

With additional portions and special assistance by Jeffrey Mark Bruce

-and-

***My First Gay Bar* by Richard Knight, Jr.**

Dugan's Bistro and the Legend of the Bearded Lady
© 2018 By Owen Keehnen

ISBN 978-0-9992172-8-3

OutTales Publishing
7406 N. Claremont #3S
Chicago, IL. 60645

Front and Back Cover Photo: Charles Shotwell
Author Photo: Andie McKenzie Meadows
Cover Design: Kirk Williamson

This book is dedicated to all those lost in the epidemic and whose legends will never be known.

Introduction: What Becomes a Legend Most?

Capturing social and cultural history is tricky business. Often, the top priority in documenting the past is an accurate account based on unbiased reporting and verifiable facts. However, with a great deal of LGBT history, especially bar history, that sort of accuracy is not always possible.

As a writer and grassroots historian, I have conducted numerous interviews over the years that tap into people's memories. I am often struck by the distance between the reality of the past and the truth of the past. The reality we remember is largely interpretive, it resides in the stories we carry and in the subjective processing of people and events.

Memory is an impression, a version of truth enhanced by hearsay, point of view, mood, selective editing, and exaggeration. Recollection meanders around a timeline without necessarily following one. Years pass. Stories distort. Lines converge and blur. Accuracy grows muddled. This tendency is in our DNA. The result is not a falsifying of the past, but the distilling of a story to its essence. This is how legends are made.

While chronicling the LGBT community and the gay disco scene in the 1970s/80s, I was exploring a population that was mostly underground, partially censored, sometimes closeted, and often under the influence of drugs and alcohol. Time has taken a great toll on memories. Many key players in the "downtown glitter scene" were lost in the AIDS epidemic; others died of natural causes, in accidents, or overdosed. They took their stories with them.

To resurrect the era, I used a framework of facts enhanced by Internet and archival exploration, newspaper recounts, fluff pieces, advertisements, lore, journals, police reports, medical records, etc. However, the goal of this book was to capture the era and life of the Bearded Lady. To achieve this meant that the foundation of this book needed to be primarily built from the memories of those who loved, and were loved by, him as well as those strangers whose memories of the Bearded Lady were central to how they recollect their own lives.

Dugan's Bistro and the Legend of the Bearded Lady is a folklore-bio of a time and place that were key in the evolution of Chicago's LGBT community. The Bearded Lady's story is a gateway to telling a larger story about the nightlife and exuberance of a "lost" generation, as well as the story of a life after that party ended.

Throughout this book my goal has been to present the Bearded Lady and the crucial times in our history that his story embodies, as best I could given the sources. Not all the memories and anecdotes may be completely accurate, but sometimes truth is greater than the sum of its actual parts.

Sometimes truth is a legend.

- Owen Keehnen, 2018.

Dugan's Bistro
and the
Legend of the Bearded Lady

Dancing Queen

The Bearded Lady (aka "BL") was heavyset with a mane of brown hair that hung halfway to his ass. His full beard frequently sparkled with glitter and his manicured nails were long. He tended to refrain from polish, but sometimes painted them dark red, purple, or black. The pinkie nail on his right hand was especially long, which often meant "scoop and sniff" in the disco era.

His make-up was theatrically gauche. Some described his make-up kit as his "box of crayons." BL was fond of kimonos and sunglasses, jewelry, 5-inch heels, parasols, and opera gloves; but his signature props were the hand fans that he used with coy abandon both on and off of the stage.

At the Bistro, BL appeared Thursday through Sunday at midnight and 2:00AM for two 15-minute shows. On special occasions he did a third show at 10:00PM. Technically, he was a theatrical dancer – though he didn't dance so much as hop and move and turn. *Forward. Side. Back. Turn. Forward.* His appeal didn't lie in his dancing skills, but in his dancing attire. BL was layered with clothes. As he moved he went through a kind of metamorphosis, shedding layers and transforming before the audience's eyes. The effect was spellbinding. BL's drag was never about glamour, but always about the reveal, and the surprise.

His performance, his act of transformation, was an apt metaphor for the newly liberated gay community and the nightlife scene at the time. His persona, both onstage and off, was one of unbridled joy, silliness, and being fabulous, not in spite of his imperfections, but because of them. BL was about possibilities and becoming. He was thrilled to be having such a glorious time and his mood was infectious. The crowds adored him.

Despite his celebrity, BL remained a mystery. The offstage life of this euphoric creature seemed unfathomable to many, until now…

Once Upon a Time...

On May 20th, 1947 there was a solar eclipse. On the same day Bob Theiss (pronounced "Tice") was born into a conservative military family in Williamsburg, New York, a suburb of Buffalo. Bob shared his birthday with James Stewart, Dolly Madison, and one of his idols, Cher.

On his father's side he was German. His paternal grandfather, Wilhelm, had arrived at Ellis Island in 1904. Throughout his life Bob's most cherished possessions were his grandfather's ring and his German passport. Bob's mother, Kathleen Margaret Traquair – "Kay" – was of Scottish and English descent and one of six children. Bob had one sister, Cynthia, seven years his senior.

As an adult, Bob rarely spoke of his childhood, but when he did he spoke of "Bobby" in the third person. "Bobby used to like sitting under the trees," "Bobby liked birthday cake," etc. Things associated with childhood were often described in that way as well. He called nursery school carts for toddlers Bobby Cars.

Later in life, Bob would share stories with friends about his mother dressing him up in pretty things when he got fussy. "When she dressed me up to play in the backyard, that always settled me down," he said.

As a child, Bob was a precocious, effeminate, quipster who was doted on by his mother. During family gatherings and holiday functions Bob preferred the company of adults. He refused to sit at the "children's table." Even then his relatives considered him a character.

His first job was working part time at a nursery; the kind of establishment with plants, not babies. He was a "helper" – a position that involved answering questions, bagging merchandise, placing the flowers onto flat trays, and/or carrying the plants to the cars of various customers. At the nursery, Bob acquired his encyclopedic knowledge of flowers and plants, an expertise he would use his entire life. He enjoyed learning new things and acquiring knowledge.

At sixteen, Bob made a list of 20 New Year's Resolutions for 1964:

1. To get greater honors
2. To have clear complexion
3. To do Good deeds and respect my parents
4. Not waste my time with people unimportant to me
5. To build and strengthen my body
6. To get my exercise
7. Not to procrastinate anymore
8. Not to feel sorry for myself
9. Use my abilities and not to waste them
10. Do more work for my parents to lessen their workload
11. To do all my homework on time and do extra credit work
12. To humble myself as well as be a friend to all
13. Go on to college and plan a summer of work, travel, relaxation, and fun for spring recess and summer vacation
14. To create better feelings around the home
15. Not be two-faced
16. To study diligently and not to waste time on unimportant things
17. To, above all, wake up and do things and go places and become a success
18. Clean my room and keep it clean
19. Be attentive
20. Keep communion, read my Bible

At the time that Bob compiled his impressive to-do list, he was attending Deveaux Prep, a posh boarding school in Niagara Falls. Despite his obvious intelligence, Bob hadn't done very well in the public school system. He later intimated that his parents took him out of public school and enrolled him at Deveaux because he was brutally teased and bullied. Bob found private school to be an improvement, but it could be snobby. He should have graduated from there in 1965, but when he was first enrolled, Deveaux administrators frowned upon his previous performance in public school. His instructors deemed it best that he repeat 9th grade.

Bob later shared with friends that there was plenty of diddling going on amongst students at the strict boarding school. He claimed that this was where he first enjoyed sex and first realized he was gay. He also asserted that Deveaux was where he developed a lifelong love of seeing men in uniform.

After Deveaux, Bob headed to the Midwest where he attended Franklin College in the town of Franklin, 25 miles south of Indianapolis. Being several hours from home in New York was an adjustment, but he liked his independence.

In 1968, after completing freshman and sophomore years at Franklin, Bob entered the Air Force. His father, a military man, may have had something to do with the decision. He always wanted to make his father proud. Bob later speculated to friends that Robert Sr. harbored hopes that the service would, "Make a man out of him."

In the Air Force, Bob worked in communications in Korea during the Vietnam War. He had a sensitive security radioman position near the Korean Demilitarized Zone in South Korea. His supervisor told him more than once that if North Korea invaded the country he would immediately have to kill Bob and then himself. Both men knew too much and it was imperative that neither of them be captured.

Bob's supervisor had no idea that Bob was harboring another big secret that had nothing to do with security. Though he performed his duties admirably, during his time in the armed forces Bob led a double life as a well-compensated hustler. He was very discreet about his side work. No "quickies" with enlisted men. Officers had the power and the money so he spent a good deal of time socializing at the officer's club. Bob preferred married officers since his talents and their situations were better matched than with a possibly talkative single man. Married officers knew how to keep the information classified.

He never had a boyfriend in the service; Bob thought that would attract too much attention. During his time in Korea, he even attempted to go to Vietnam on "R & R" because of the potential for money from hustling, but the request was denied. He didn't pursue the issue. Given his unbridled love of shopping, money was always a necessity.

Bob viewed Seoul as a great sprawling retail opportunity. He relished visiting the stores and markets and bargaining for various items. He loved exploring the city and meeting the people of Seoul. In a matter of months, he seemed to know everyone, including Kim Dae-Jung. [Dae-Jung later became the President of South Korea (1998-2003) and was awarded the Nobel Peace Prize in 2000.] Bob was also thrilled that, during his time in Korea, his May 20th birthday was celebrated as Buddha's birthday.

Following his honorable discharge from the service in 1970, Bob headed to San Francisco. Talk of the Summer of Love had sparked his curiosity about the City by the Bay, but that had occurred three years earlier. During his extended vacation, he tried to see everything San Francisco had to offer. For a gay man in 1970, that was plenty. The city was as raunchy as he'd hoped, but different than he expected. Bob enjoyed himself, but San Francisco didn't feel like home. After a couple weeks, he headed to Chicago.

In the Windy City Bob found a place in West Lakeview, a couple of blocks from his beloved Aunt Sophie Shoemaker [1904-1996]. Sophie wasn't actually Bob's aunt, but an older female relative. Sophie helped Bob get acclimated and find a job. He was first employed doing office work at Illinois Bell in Evanston and then more office work at Evanston Hospital. He found both jobs mind-numbing. Office work was not the sort of thing he had in mind when he moved to Chicago. Bob wanted excitement and adventure.

As he grew more comfortable with the city, Bob began frequenting the bars. Around the same time he began experimenting with a semi-feminine appearance. He would wear what he referred to as "accents" – a wild coat or a big skirt or a glittery brooch – things of that nature. The response was good. When he started combining items, like earrings and a skirt, the response was better. The attention felt good. As with most everything, Bob wanted more.

His look was very unconventional for the typical drag of the period, but that didn't concern him. Bob was bearded and hairy and loved every curl and follicle of his fur. Never one to compromise, he instead was inspired to adopt the old Bearded Lady circus persona. He flipped the gender of the archetype and adapted it for the club scene.

In San Francisco he'd been inspired by Hibiscus and the avant-garde theatre group, the Cockettes with their heavy makeup and facial hair. He told a friend, "I knew those bitches [the Cockettes] and I brought that look to Chicago." Bob took that spark of inspiration as his starting point, but made it his own.

From the start, Bob and the Bearded Lady were different people. The Bearded Lady was a creation, a character, and a performance. Though he was often called she, both Bob and BL used and preferred the pronoun he. BL never corrected people, he was pleased people were talking about him.

I Love the Night Life!

In the early 1970s, gay nightlife in Chicago was flourishing in spite of years of raids and police harassment. Common charges in the periodic *vice sweeps* were "Disorderly Conduct" or "Public Indecency"; both were subjective infractions that meant any display of affection among same-sex couples, even holding hands, was a crime. Buying someone a drink was considered solicitation. Bartenders serving an undercover officer might be busted for solicitation. If the allegations were met with the slightest protest, a charge of resisting arrest was added. Police cruisers sometimes parked outside gay bars with their lights flashing to intimidate and deter patrons. It didn't.

The River North neighborhood was fairly dodgy at the time, making it perfect for a vibrant LGBT nightlife. Parking was plentiful. Very few people lived in the area, so noise on the street brought minimal complaints. After business hours during the week and from 5:00PM on Friday until Monday morning, the River North area was a gay playground.

For the next few years, River North would be home to numerous LGBT bars and clubs including: Sundays, Togetherness, King's Ransom, the Trip, Alfie's, the Ritz, the Redoubt, and Ozone. The New Flight was the main hustler bar in the area. Iconic gay leather bar, the Gold Coast, was a block away from the legendary drag bar, the Baton Show Lounge. In River North, bar hopping was the thing to do. Many folks remember coming to the area for the first time and being astounded that there were that many gay people in the world. In those magical few blocks, there was an overwhelming sense of community and the feeling that when we came together, nothing could harm us.

By 1972 Bob had started frequenting P.Q.'s, a popular disco in the area. He first arrived at the nightspot in platforms, fishnets, and a tartan kilt and quickly got a reputation for outrageousness. When a new disco to end all discos was scheduled to open in May of 1973, the owner and promoter would remember him…

Best Disco in Town

The Bistro was the brainchild of 26 year-old entrepreneur and party man Edward L. Davison, a.k.a. "Eddie Dugan." In the press, Eddie was quoted as saying he used the name, "for reasons too long and complicated to explain." Dugan saw the trend in music and felt a change happening in the bars: the gay community was coming out of the shadows and proclaiming their recent liberation. Dancing for same-sex couples – which had been illegal a decade earlier - was becoming a big part of the celebration of those newfound freedoms.

Although same sex dancing was no longer a crime in Illinois, the police were free to interpret it any way they chose, which usually meant "Public Indecency." That began to change in April of 1970 when Chicago's LGBT community fought and organized to end this sort of persecution with picketing and protests outside the Normandy Inn.

A Gay Lib leaflet circulated outside the bar read: *"The oppressive atmosphere of the Normandy must be removed. The right to dance, any tempo, any style, is thus a crucial step towards our personal and collective liberation."* The club's owners obtained a license that permitted same-sex dancing in approximately two weeks' time. At last the community seemed to have come into its own and people were ready to celebrate the hard-won victory – and **party**.

Two and a half years later Eddie Dugan, who had been working as a bartender at Broadway Sam's, went with his boyfriend, Ron Veltman, to P.Q.'s. Eddie was accustomed to the dark, filthy, and windowless look of gay bars during the period. P.Q.'s offered the expected: a long bar in front and some tables and chairs. But the club also featured some things that were unusual, like a series of illuminated display cases with assorted miniature vignettes in the front seating area as well as an enormous oil painting of Mae West in the basement.

The main draw at P.Q.'s, however, was the music. The back of the disco had a horseshoe bar with a DJ booth above. That fateful night a DJ was spinning records and the tiled dance floor was packed. Observing the crowd, Ron turned to Eddie and shouted over the music, "If you open a place like this, but five times the size, you'll be a millionaire." That comment resonated. Dugan had worked in enough gay bars by then (Shari's, Ruthie's, and his gig at Broadway Sam's) to realize he could offer patrons more than what they expected. He could give people something they didn't even realize they wanted.

Eddie, Ron, and friend/roommate Richard Cooke, looked at several possible locations before choosing the four-story building at 420 N. Dearborn formerly occupied by Le Bistro, a French restaurant with specialties that included quiche Loraine, raw oysters, and steak au poivre. The location was ideal. Seizing the opportunity, Eddie borrowed $5,000 from his parents, Edward Sr. and Helen, to match the $5,000 acquired from his business partners, Sam and Flo Levine, and signed a 10-year lease.

When Eddie assumed ownership and first entered the building, the restaurant had been left "as is" with plates and glasses still on the table. Oyster shells were glued to the back wall. Dishes and chairs were in the back along with a huge stove. Red-flocked wallpaper covered the walls in the front room. There were velvet drapes and an array of large oil paintings.

The new layout of the Bistro was planned using a shoebox lined with foil to simulate the nightclub, but Eddie didn't completely overhaul the interior right away. Renovations would come once the bar started earning money. He chose to keep the restaurant name, and even the restaurant sign. He just removed "Le" and added his "stage name" Dugan, above the restaurant name. The gay community's newest nightspot – "Dugan's Bistro" – was born.

Chuck Renslow, Chicago businessman and owner of the Gold Coast, was quoted in his biography, *Leatherman: The Legend of Chuck Renslow*, as saying, "When Eddie opened up the Bistro around the corner from the Gold Coast, [he] was very green as far as opening up a bar, and he had no political clout. He asked if I would help him. I said I would be glad to; it would bring more people to the area around Hubbard, Clark, and Illinois [Streets]. I went to [Cook County politician] George Dunne, and had him pull some strings and got Eddie his license. In those days, if you knew somebody, you got your license right away."

With money finally coming in, Dugan began transforming the space. He took up the carpet and redid the floors. Up the three central stairs was the dance floor and off of that was another room with tables and chairs for extra seating. Some of the original red-flocked wallpaper was left on the walls and an entire wall of gold-framed oil paintings remained in the lower bar.

Lesbian bar manager and owner Marge Summit recalled that moment in Chicago nightlife history. "I was at P.Q.'s. I liked it there because it was men and women. That place was always packed. *Always*. I heard the Bistro was opening down the street and I told the owner, 'This place is going to take away your business' and he said, 'No, we'll be OK.' Once the Bistro opened, you could go through P.Q.'s with a pool cue sideways and not hit anyone." Shortly after P.Q.'s closed, Marge took over the space and turned it into the lesbian disco, MS.

Eddie Dugan had been blessed with a Midas touch; only instead of gold; he turned everything he touched into a party. As a bar owner Dugan had an invaluable gift, a charismatic knack for approaching each person at the bar and within two minutes, making that person think they were the reason he was happy, they were the reason he came to work that night, and they were even the reason he opened the Bistro in the first place. Then, he would move on to the next person, and convince them of the same thing.

With Eddie at the helm, the Bistro soon became the premiere club of Chicago, ground zero of the downtown scene. Bistro regulars realized they were part of something special and called themselves Bistro Bunnies or Duganites.

The disco scene was growing, and the Bistro was leading the way. The sound, the concept, the ambiance; the Bistro pioneered ideas that eventually became the disco norm. Dugan's *Bistrotheque* set the mold for a new kind of club defined by decadence, outrageousness, and excitement. After years of repression, it was time for abandon. Though it's often referred to as the Studio 54 of the Midwest, the Bistro's opening *pre*dated that iconic New York nightspot by four years.

When the Bistro opened in May of 1973, Donn Abbinanti reported, "Everyone in the city showed up in costume to pay their respects (even P.Q. & Lee from Coming Out). Every bar sent ambassadors to see the dynamite job done on the disco by its designers… One of the most together BOOGIE ROOMS this city has seen."

Discussing the opening of the popular nightspot, Abbinanti added, "The police were at it again, the first Saturday the Bistro was open. If you didn't know better you'd think it was a Film Company on location. Police were running from all directions. Squad Cars were everywhere. And then it was over. Nothing happened! Why can't the city put the police and gasoline for the squads to better use than to harass the Gay Community? Maybe someday!"

Some may have been surprised by the immediate popularity and success of the Bistro, but not Eddie Dugan. He knew how to throw a big fabulous bash and the Bistro was all about having a party every single night. The pace and the flash – the disco era – was *made* for Eddie Dugan. He drove a silver 450SL Mercedes-Benz convertible with the license plate "ELD 46" that stood for Edward L. Dugan and the year he was born. Years later, he would consider Alicia Bridges' 1978 hit *I Love the Nightlife* to be his signature song because it captured his general outlook on life. Eddie was the undisputed master of high-energy nightlife and the "King of the Downtown Glitter Scene."

Despite the demure club motto ("The Bistro, Nice People doing nice things for Nice People") outrageousness ruled. Patrons never knew who or what they might see. The surprise element heightened the anticipation of going there because staying home meant missing something people would be talking about for weeks. And, from the beginning, people were talking about the Bearded Lady.

Fame (Remember My Name)

For nine years the Bistro reigned as the hottest club in Chicago – a genuine nightlife phenomenon – and above the door on the marquee, as well as on the club's business cards and matchbooks, it said "Dugan's Bistro, the Home of the Bearded Lady."

With the Bistro as his platform, BL became a star. Comedienne Phyllis Diller applauded him. Bruce Vilanch referred to him as "Chicago's Living Legend." *Gay Life* columnist Ron Herizon hailed his infectious lunacy as "Chicago's answer to Bette Milder." He posed for noted photographers like Chuck Shotwell and Marc Hauser. Glitz and glitter artist, Bob "Windy City Warhol" Fischer, who called his art bizzarte, immortalized him in an oil painting.

BL was a bona fide celebrity. People shouted to him from passing cars and called his name from department store balconies. On the street some people asked for a picture, for an autograph, or both. He was always thrilled to oblige. He was born for this because BL adored his public as much as they adored him. He was routinely featured in the gay and straight press alike for any number of reasons. He attended dozens of nightlife events, play openings, fundraisers, and restaurant debuts. He wrestled in cake batter for charity and ended the match by licking his opponent into submission. He was frequently a featured entertainer at the Mr. Windy City contests and a popular guest at film festivals. People joked that he'd show up at the opening of an envelope.

On New Year's Eve of 1974, he arrived by limo at the "black towel optional" opening of the Music Hall at the legendary Man's Country bathhouse where he performed for the mostly naked crowd. BL was paid handsomely to perform and "carry on" at private parties before hitting the Bistro stage at midnight.

In 1975, at the showing of *The Pig and I: A Love Story* for the Chicago International Film Festival, the film's porky star was squealing in the lobby. Eager to hog some of the spotlight, BL picked up the piglet and put it next to his face as the cameras flashed. The image of BL and the pig was all over the papers, and television, the following day.

Aaron Gold's 1975 Tower Ticker column in the *Chicago Tribune* dished about BL being listed among a roster of celebrities attending a sneak preview of *Tommy* at the State-Lake Theater. "Tina Turner, who plays the Acid Queen, definitely will be on hand... Zsa Zsa and Eva Gabor, Stefanie Powers, Bobby; The Bearded Lady, the Who's John Entwistle, and possibly Ann-Margret (if her plane arrives on time) will get together later at Arnie's for a Hollywood type glitter party complete with Bally Wizard pinball machines."

In an era when much of the Gay Pride Parade was banners and beer trucks, BL was always a highlight. When he rode by on the Bistro float, the crowd went wild. He grew so excited by the adulation that he would shriek and cackle with delight. Of the ten minutes of footage that exists from Chicago's 1976 Pride Parade by filmmaker Tom Palazzolo, a healthy portion is devoted to BL making his way into position on a float while carrying a Fiorucci shopping bag and wearing a layered mini-sundress with white stockings, satin opera gloves, and a half-veil.

At a David Bowie concert, BL received media coverage after arriving in an enormous polka dot ante-bellum gown, with a zebra print shawl, and a huge southern belle hat festooned with ermine tails hanging from the brim. Over the hat was a surfeit of black bridal netting that he tied beneath his chin in an oversized bow. He carried an enormous silver fan and his beard sparkled with glitter.

The attention was like a drug. Each press photo and every column mention prompted BL to be more outrageous in his public appearances. He showed up in costumes evermore over-the-top and sporting an *I have arrived* attitude. He was always ready to cause a commotion; which he did at a film screening from which he was turned away because his enormous headpiece was both too high *and* too wide for people to see around.

On July 11, 1977, he was prominently pictured in a *Time Magazine* piece on the punk music phenomenon in America. The photo was taken while waiting in line at a concert. In the shot

BL wore silver platform shoes with black and gold ankle ribbons, silvery hose with garters, a leopard print hot pants/top combo, gold workout belt, black coat, pink sunglasses and a biker hat with a pink floral purse slung over his shoulder. His leopard print top was open to his waist, revealing two slabs of meat on his chest that had been fashioned into a bra. When *Time* hit the stands BL was over the moon. He came onto the Bistro stage that night wearing a red, white, and blue sequin outfit with lit sparklers in his hair. As the music started he began shrieking and spinning in a euphoric whirl. Eventually he stopped and screamed, "Your Mother has made *Time Magazine!*"

On Oct 1 the same year, BL headlined a show in Toronto with the popular punk band "Oh Those Pants" at the Ontario College of Art, which was the center of punk rock in the city. On the accompanying t-shirts he received top billing: BL in huge black letters against a white background. Within the black initials were the words: "THE BEARDED LADY and OH! THOSE PANTS!" A pair of lips completed the artwork. The wide press coverage of the event thrilled him.

Even the December 1979 issue of *Penthouse* magazine mentioned him. Once he became "a name," BL had various agents and representatives who tried to book him on *The Tonight Show* and other programs. Although he garnered attention and was undeniably a phenomenon, his performance did not transcend the moment. His persona was too scattered, too unpolished, too unpredictable, and maybe a little too gay for the mass palate. Middle America was not ready to have this avant-garde sensation in their living rooms.

But it didn't matter. For those who knew BL – or knew of him – his live personae was so commanding that, when discussing the opening of Chicago's chicest new clothing boutique, a *Chicago Sun-Times* writer reported, with tongue in cheek precision, "The Bearded Lady...was not there." He had achieved so much notoriety that even *Chicago Tribune* arts columnist Claudia Cassidy mentioned his arrival at an event in her popular half-hour program on WFMT radio. Hearing his name uttered by "Acidy Cassidy" – of all people – BL felt he had, indeed, arrived – in more ways than one.

Dance (Disco Heat)

Entering the Bistro, patrons were simultaneously hit by the heat and the beat. For some the first order of business was checking a coat; for others it was grabbing a cocktail; a few went directly to score some drugs. There were several dealers on site, and a couple on staff. Each had their special sections and selections.

Readily available "mood enhancing" substances included marijuana, Seconal, Valium, the veterinary drug PCP ("Angel Dust"), and LSD. The three most popular were cocaine, MDA, and Quaaludes. Many partygoers were also fond of inhalants such as ampules of amyl nitrate, poppers, and "snaps/snappers" aka pharmaceutical poppers.

For an exceptional high on the dance floor, some patrons soaked the knotted end of a bandana with ethyl chloride and danced with the knot held between their teeth and the other end of the rag hanging out of their mouth. At the Bistro, ethyl could be purchased from several dealers on site for around $10-$15 a bottle.

Periodically, there would be a drug "incident" after someone took too much of something or mixed the wrong drugs. Only one known fatality due to a drug overdose ever occurred at the Bistro. The person was found slumped in a booth and taken out a side door. A dead body inside the club would require shutting down the bar so a coroner's investigation could be launched. No one wanted that. If the body was found outside it would be just as dead as if found in a booth. The overdose – though tragic – was no reason to stop the party for the living (and paying) patrons inside. As cynical as it may seem in retrospect, the Bistro was – first and foremost – a business. And illegal drug use inside clubs happened everywhere, all the time. Nothing would be gained by allowing the Bistro's reputation to be tarnished.

Many of the people who danced and worked at the Bistro were on some sort of mood enhancing drug – often two or more. But, make no mistake; the Bistro *itself* was the real drug. Paying the cover and crossing the threshold was akin to entering a different universe. And, from the beginning, music was a big part of that journey.

Ron Veltman – Eddie Dugan's boyfriend, whose original encouragement prompted Eddie to open the club – was one of the Bistro's first DJs. He was gorgeous. Cosmopolitan. Suave. Gracious. Always impeccably groomed and dressed, Ron projected an air of mystery that many Bistro regulars found irresistible. He commanded the two turntables in the days before the advent of mixing; and he had developed great instincts for sensing what the crowd wanted to hear. Ron had a blue police car light mounted outside the DJ booth. When he played *Armed and Extremely Dangerous* by First Choice, he'd flip the "ON" switch for the light. Hearing the opening beats and seeing the flashing blue cut through the room made the crowd go crazy. The squad flasher was lost in one of the bar's many renovations. Some sort of renewal or improvement always seemed to be in progress at the Bistro. With the bar's reputation set, Ron eventually moved from resident DJ into a management position at the Bistro.

In late 1975 rumors were rife that the Bistro and the Gold Coast were closing down and the area was slated for urban renewal. The fears proved premature. An article in the *Chicago Gay Crusader* from January 1976 read: "The Bistro is still in business, despite all the rumors to the contrary, and they're doing remodeling. The Tube, it's to be called. The back room of this popular disco is being remodeled into a real wild 'cruise' room, with silver and glitter and whatnot." The wallpaper they added featured silver palm trees. The renovation included adding three tiers of black stairs to one side of the main floor bar. The stairs were for sitting, posing, and cruising, and they also offered a great view of the go-go boys on the two circular dance platforms.

After the extensive 1979 renovation, the decor was deep green with a layout as follows: At the entrance was a display board with all the "activities" of the week; drink specials, performers scheduled to appear, etc. Past the entryway was the main room on the lower level. On the left were two banquettes on risers to one side. Beyond the banquettes was the game room with a couple pool tables (and usually some hustlers), some early video games, and pinball machines. At one time the wall behind the pool tables was covered with the seats of numerous pairs of blue jean cut offs stuffed to look like real butts. On another wall was a pay phone beside a cigarette machine. *Come to Marlboro Country*. For most of the Bistro run, cigarettes were seventy-five cents a pack.

On the right when entering the club was an enormous walk around "racetrack" bar, ideal for cruising. Here, the circle-and-pose style of pick-up was practiced until it became an art form. Over the bar was a custom-made light fixture comprised of hundreds of clear Lucite tubes of varying lengths, each housing white a strand of Italian Lights. On one wall was a pair of flashing red neon lips inspired by the enormous Magikist lips sign along the expressway. On the opposite wall a flashing sign that said, "Boogie." Actually, the sign said "Boogie Boogie" but the two signs blinked in alternation. In late afternoon and early evening, this front area was the only part of the bar open to the public.

Beyond the front bar was a frosted glass wall with "Dugan's Bistro" etched into the glass in the club's signature font. Past the decorative glass were the coat check, another cigarette machine, and the bathrooms – which were a social center at the Bistro because, after some sweaty dancing, friends would gather in the bathrooms to get high and keep their look happening by blow-drying their hair with the swivel nozzle of the hand dryers.

The bathrooms were also a popular place for those who were unable to arrive as "themselves" and who brought make-up and wigs and whatnot and got ready in the stalls. Before leaving the Bistro most of those club devotees went back to the restroom and removed everything. Outrageous was not a safe look for those returning to uncertain neighborhoods or intolerant homes.

After the bathrooms and coat check, patrons climbed a set of three wide steps to the second level – ground zero of the Bistro – the dance floor. On the dance floor, people did poppers, smoked joints, and sometimes even had sex. Orgasms and bacchanalian abandon were a welcome part of the party. Little was off limits at the Bistro.

Elevated and to the left of the dance floor was the DJ booth where the bar's award-winning spin-master and music-mixer, Lou DiVito, created his magic. As a signal that the dance floor was open, bar backs removed the Japanese screen at the top of the stairs. Lou frequently opened the dance floor with one of his favorite low-key songs, *TSOP (The Sound of Philadelphia)* by MFSB.

DiVito had attended the Harrington Institute of Design. In 1974, he was helping out at the Bistro and was in the booth when Ron Veltman was promoted to a management position. Lou was a self-taught DJ. He'd put on one record, then another, learning the art – and the power – of music mixing as he went along; eventually incorporating the technological innovations that came to shape his signature sound.

The smoked glass on Lou's three-sided DJ booth slanted forward. The dark glass made it easier to do drugs inside without being seen. The booth had a half door. Lou opened the top half if people wanted to talk, but he mostly kept the lower half locked because he took his job seriously. When he was working, Lou often didn't want to engage. Music took him into his own world.

Inside the booth two turntables were suspended from the ceiling. The set-up prevented the records from skipping when the room shook – and, with hundreds of people dancing at the same time, the Bistro shook a lot. Before they got around to elevating the DJ booth and suspending the turntables, there were signs along the dance floor that read "No Jumping."

Beside the turntables was Lou's special mixer with an enormous control knob. The device blended songs, altering the volume and mix as one song flowed into the other. Lou once explained that he blended the music to create a story. His objective was to take the dancers, and the dance floor, on a journey.

In front of Lou in the DJ booth was his record bin with current songs in heavy rotation. Behind him were two other bins of records, songs he was working in or out of his sets. On a shelf between the bins were Lou's essentials: his Carmex, his comb, and his cocaine. On the wall above the shelf was an enormous poster of Diana Ross' *Love Hangover* record cover. In order to decipher his albums in the dim light of the booth, Lou wrote the title and the BPMs (beats per minute) of each record on the sleeve in a black marker.

Those who knew Lou DiVito best describe him as a complicated, talented, and fun loving man. He loved being a DJ and controlling the mood of the room. But outside of the glass DJ booth, Lou could be socially awkward and was painfully shy with strangers. Friends sometimes called him, "The Hermit DJ." Music was Lou's voice.

In a 1977 issue of *GayLife*, Lou was asked if life as the top DJ at Chicago's "super gay discotheque" was as glamorous as it seemed. He replied, "Actually it can be very lonely. You work five nights a week so it leaves little chance for meeting someone or socializing. It can also be very frustrating because if you see someone on the dance floor who you might like to meet you don't have the time to go out and talk to him. The real crusher is seeing that same person approached by someone else and watching them leave the bar together."

Asked once about his secret for picking music, Lou said, "I play what the customers want to hear. Anything that I know will get them up to dance. They come here to party and I want to make sure they have a good time." He liked to say, the music was about the crowd, not about the DJ. Further enshrining his legendary status, in 1979 Lou DiVito became Chicago radio's first "hot mixer" after signing an exclusive contract with WDAI to produce custom half hour mixes for the station. Management at the station buzzed, "Lou captures the excitement of his disco and makes it sizzle." In addition to being the number one DJ at the Bistro, Lou also wrote the *Disco Beat* column in *Gay Chicago Magazine*.

Billboard Magazine named Lou Regional Disco DJ of the Year

for the Chicago Area for two consecutive years. One year, the Queen of Disco, Donna Summer, presented him with the award. In 1979 the Bistro was named Top Club at the Chicago Disco Awards held at the Aragon Ballroom with Eddie accepting the award. Eddie and Lou were both in attendance to be honored at the 1980 Chicago Music Awards. That night the Bistro won Best Gay Disco and Lou came in second as Best DJ.

Record companies and promoters courted Lou and recording artists sought his stamp of approval. He was honored with a gold record for the promotion of the Patrick Hernandez hit, *Born to Be Alive*. According to the *Chicago Disco Guide* for May of 1979, "Lou is responsible for breaking Gloria Gaynor's *I Will Survive* when Polydor Records was pushing the other side, *Substitute*." Even disco icon Sylvester had a crush on him. Lou was a bona fide disco god.

Ambiance was a huge part of the Bistro's popularity and allure. The club always felt fresh and fun. The edgy effects and lighting at the Bistro were mostly the work of techno-genius Thomas "TL" Noble who first came to the bar at 19 as a go-go boy. However, the sexy dancer in platform tennis shoes, tube socks, gym shorts, and muscle t-shirt had more to offer than the obvious. Noble had creative vision, a wonderful imagination, and an incredible knack for the "feel" of the evening.

TL loved making the Bistro a visually transformative experience. He drew ideas on bar napkins and discussed them with Lou, Eddie and the building's engineer. With Eddie's complete support, and sometime assistance, Noble's exceptional visions were brought to life. When TL decided he wanted the dance floor to look like the inside of a gigantic cave, he worked for two days to construct "stalactites" out of plastic that were mounted on the lights. Another time he transformed the bar into a firehouse. The Bistro even became "outer space" with suspended planets and shooting star lighting effects. Being a talented performer as well, Noble eventually moved from lighting and design to talent management when he was promoted to Bistro Stage Manager.

In the DJ booth, one of Lou and TL's favorite pastimes was to play with the White Rain Light. When spotting a cute guy, a meaty man-basket, or an exceptional ass on the dance floor, the two sent a solid beam of light onto the guy or his crotch or his butt. A White Rain shaft of light on an employee was a signal to come to the DJ booth. It usually meant that TL or Lou needed a break or a drink.

The dance floor at the Bistro was in the forefront of many things that became the discotheque norm. There were flashing rainbow-colored lights; multi-colored "Mars" alarm beacons on poles aside intermittent black lights; and chase lights edging and veining the dance floor, sometimes racing in tandem, other times in opposite directions. Rather than being raised, the dance floor at the Bistro was sunken, with risers around its perimeter that housed additional Mars lights.

The Bistro had nine mirror balls. Strategically placed confetti cannons periodically erupted with bursts of glitter. Four mortar guns shot foam stars, moons, and planets onto the dance floor. Sometimes it rained streamers, and other times it snowed. To prepare a "snowstorm," an employee went upstairs to "fluff the snow" in the garbage drums before the pellets were released.

Other nights fog would drift across the floor. Dry ice was kept in drums in the basement. To create fog, the ice was dropped into hot water with the resultant mist sent through tubes that emerged from three outlets hidden in the risers around the dance floor. In no time, a heavy cloud would envelop the dance floor, move over the risers, and roll down the three stairs into the entry bar.

When the music was playing and the lights were going – with snow falling or a fog encasing the room – the Bistro was often described as "otherworldly" and "heavenly." One patron called those times the finest moments of his life.

Beside Lou's DJ roost was the upper back seating area of the club with five banquettes – a private space known as the VIP Lounge. It was there that "Planet Janet" ruled as the cocktail waitress. If you needed cocaine or Quaaludes (aka disco biscuits) to enhance the evening, Janet could help with that too. She was a force of nature. If you put a coat on a banquette in her section without asking, Janet might pick it up and throw it onto the dance floor. Sometimes she even poured grenadine down the inside of the sleeves of the errant outerwear so when the person put on their coat the deep-red syrup got all over their arms. Planet Janet was yet another a Bistro *original*.

Janet and back bartender Jimmy Knight sometimes "play fought." To dramatize the battle, Janet held a bit of grenadine in her mouth. When Jimmy pretended to smash her face onto the bar, Janet then came up with what appeared to be blood running from her mouth and down her chin. Eddie didn't discourage theatrics from his staff. He knew people would talk about it, and when they did, they'd say it happened at the Bistro.

Celebrities were something else people talked about seeing at the Bistro. An impressive roster of stars came through its doors. Bette Midler, Jacqueline Bisset, Alexander Godonov, or Ashford & Simpson might be seen on the dance floor. At the bar people might catch a glimpse of Billy Preston, Halston (with an entourage of models), Diana Ross, or Candice Bergen sipping a drink. Other stars who came to Chicago's premiere disco included Rick James, Seka, Barry Manilow, Minnie Riperton, Bill Wyman, Divine, John Waters, Margaux Hemingway, Rip Taylor, Liza Minnelli, Rock Hudson, Bill Blass, Harry Hamlin, Diane Von Furstenberg, Richard Pryor, Chaka Khan, Paul Lynde, Liv Ullmann, the New York Dolls, Al Pacino, Tina Turner, Ryan O'Neal, Dolph Lundgren, Gene Siskel, Roger Ebert, Cheap Trick, Brian Dennehy, Barbara Eden, Charles Nelson Reilly, Bianca Jagger, Senator Edward Kennedy, Elton John, Charo, Andy Warhol, Governor Dan Walker, and Wayland Flowers and Madame.

On any given night, patrons might see a Beach Boy, a Village person, a Pointer Sister, or a Gibb Brother. All celebrities were welcome – even the nationally known film critic who was fond of getting uproariously drunk and abusive at the downstairs bar.

Celebrities did not intimidate the Bearded Lady because he considered himself one. In 1974 when Rudolf Nureyev was in town with the National Ballet of Canada, he came to the Bistro. The *Chicago Tribune* reported that BL approached Nureyev and asked him to dance. "... Nureyev said he had just danced two shows and was tired. The Bearded Lady told him he'd just danced two shows, too, but he wasn't too tired to dance."

One time members of Led Zeppelin took BL and coworkers, including TL Noble, Danny "Dee Dee" Celebron, and Peter Bellinder, out to breakfast at the Oak Tree Restaurant – a favorite late-night, post-club hangout. The band members, especially Zeppelin founder Jimmy Paige, found the entire thing fascinating. The evening's revelry ended with Robert Plant getting his long hair tangled in the giant metal oak tree sculpture that hung from a wall at the back of the restaurant.

In November of 1977, the week before Thanksgiving, *The Turning Point* opened in Chicago. Shirley MacLaine was in town promoting the film and was coming to the Bistro that evening. In her honor, BL performed *Turkey Lake* wearing a tutu, accompanied by a live turkey (also in a tutu), on stage. Unknown to BL, two Bistro employees had fed the turkey a laxative so when BL picked up his feathered dance partner and spun it around, there was an additional surprise. BL wasn't thrilled with the shitty outcome, but was elated to discover he was the talk of the town the following week. A firm believer in *more is more*; the following year's Thanksgiving showstopper had BL performing in a pen filled with live turkeys.

In December 1977, Bette Midler was performing at Park West in the midst of a huge snowstorm. Midler was one of BL's favorite entertainers so during the performance, BL approached the stage in full regalia to give Bette a bouquet of flowers. Seeing him, Bette stopped mid-song and said, "Oh Honey, you look like shit!" The comment brought the house down.

A remarkable number of disco stars also appeared at the Bistro to promote their songs. The roster included Gloria Gaynor, Candi Staton (*Young Hearts Run Free*), Sylvester, Evelyn Thomas (*I Want to Make it On My Own*), Fonda Rae (the *Deputy of Love* girl), Viola Wills (*Let's Love Now*), Loleatta Holloway (*Hit and Run, Love Sensation*), Linda Clifford (*If My Friends Could See Me Now*), Millie Jackson (*We Got to Hit it Off, House for Sale*), Angela Clemmons (*Give Me Just a Little More Time*), Carol Jiani (*Hit n' Run Lover*), Judy Clayton (*Love's Gonna Find You*), Deborah Washington (*The Letter*), the Weather Girls (Sylvester's back-up singers when they were "Two Tons o' Fun"), and many others.

Since record promoters often picked up the tab, booking acts was fairly inexpensive. Sometimes the musical acts weren't even announced. Eddie knew the element of surprise was a key component to being a top club. A disco act might spontaneously appear on stage and do a couple songs. Patrons felt "anything might happen" at the Bistro for good reason. It worked to everyone's favor and only fueled the Bistro's epic journey into the Disco Stratosphere.

Who's That Lady?

In the corner, on the right of the VIP Lounge, was a small stage which was nothing more than 4' x 8' piece of reinforced plywood mounted on posts and elevated approximately four feet from the dance floor. The stage was accessed from the rear by a few steps with a door at the top, which had a mirrored back and opened directly onto the mirrored stage. As a result the stage resembled a music box. This platform was the domain of the Bearded Lady.

Thursday through Sunday at midnight and 2:00AM the music would end, the flashing lights would go still, and people would stop dancing. The Bistro crowd knew what was coming. The opening chords of *Love's Theme* by Barry White's Love Unlimited Orchestra would begin. A spotlight would illuminate the stage. BL would appear, oftentimes with his back to the audience. (A move and practice he referred to as "giving back.") His hips would start to sway to the music. The crowd responded with cheers and whistles. As the shouts escalated in anticipation, BL would turn. He would be wearing sunglasses with the rest of his face mostly hidden behind a hand fan. *Love's Theme* would segue into BL's other signature number, *Who's That Lady?* by the Isley Brothers. As the song moved into its first stanza:

> *Who's that lady? Who's that lady?*
> *Beautiful lady, who's that lady?*
> *Lovely lady, who's that lady?*
> *Real fine lady, who's that lady?*

The crowd would begin to chant, "Who's that Lady?" In response, BL would slowly lower his cat-eye sunglasses to look over the crowd. The audience would erupt. As the song progressed, the layers of clothing would start to be shed. BL was fond of twirling each removed garment a few times before casting it aside.

The third number in BL's set was typically a popular hit of the day. Although the third song varied, the one thing that remained relatively constant was BL's unfamiliarity with the lyrics. The crowd didn't care. They didn't expect BL to lip synch. That wasn't what this illusion – this visual *explosion* – was about. The crowd loved him even more for not knowing the words.

Accompanying all this were the screams. With each layer of clothing removed, BL shrieked with delight. In response, the crowd screamed and stomped their feet. With each layer the cries escalated. As the frenzy grew, BL broke from his sometimes flirty and sometimes demure stage presence to scream or cackle in reply. The cries on both sides increased. BL had the rare distinction of being a club act that needed the dance music to resume in order to calm the revved up crowd.

BL's clothing layers were mostly comprised of thrift store housedresses, but always included a few surprises. A poncho might be removed to reveal a housedress, and then another housedress. With another series of moves he would be in a jumpsuit, and after another turn he might be wearing gauchos and a peasant blouse. Another housedress. A slip. A nightie. A corset. A bustier. The number of layers and the amount of clothing BL was able to carry on his body was astonishing. He usually ended his act in a one-piece lady's bathing suit with his hairy legs and body on display.

The main criterion for his outfits, aside from the final reveal of the swimsuit, were that they have buttons, snaps, Velcro, or zippers. No item of clothing could go over his head because BL often wore some sort of headdress or hair extravagance. His mane was the base for each creation and things were built up from there. *Size mattered.* BL's hair and beard were adorned with lawn ornaments, blow-up toys, knitting needles, fresh flowers (poinsettia for the holidays), kitchen utensils, sex toys, a birdcage with a stuffed bird inside, lampshades, doll parts, flags, pink flamingoes, plastic fruit, a fishing pole, and countless other items. Once he even wore a sparkly gold rotary phone on his head with the receiver hovering in space and an attached conversation bubble that said, "Hello."

Dancing in a hot club, wearing layers of clothes, and being overweight ("zaftig" was what BL would say), it's not surprising that he sweated profusely. Rather than being a negative, the sloppiness was merely another aspect of his glorious imperfection. His celebration of being himself made others feel comfortable. The sweating also helped explain why hand fans became his props-of-choice. Despite his sweating, BL's make-up, which he wore thick, rarely smeared.

In a 2001 interview with Sukie de la Croix for *Windy City Times*, Rick Karlin recalled BL: "He was totally outrageous on stage, very strange. I remember him coming on with six or seven dresses on, and he would take layer after layer after layer off, and he always had a fan and he fanned himself. He had big false eyelashes, big red lips and a full beard...He looked like Abbie Hoffman doing drag."

Occasionally BL's costumes and props were thematic. For the holidays he wore a Christmas tree dress with blinking lights that plugged into an onstage socket. Sweating profusely and incorporating electricity into his outfit carried a risk. More than once, BL suffered burns due to the combination. Performance fashion sometimes meant suffering for his art – and he had the scars to prove it. BL accessorized his yuletide attire with Santa earrings, tinsel accessories, and ornaments pinned to his dress and hanging from his hair and beard.

At graduation time he appeared in a cap and gown with pencils, diploma, a team pennant, and an inkwell hidden in his beard and hair. When schools around the city were celebrating prom, BL performed in a white satin creation with lots of tulle. The seams in his prom dress had Italian lights stitched in, which pulsated to the disco beat. On his head was a five-branch candelabrum. By the end of the night he complained of a sore neck from wearing the heavy brass candleholder on his head all evening.

Sometimes the themes behind his attire were less obvious. BL once danced to Linda Clifford's *If My Friends Could See Me Now* wearing a long pink gown and a Papier-mâché cow head. The explanation for the fashion choice was in the lyrics:

What a set up! Holy cow!
They'd never believe it.
If my friends could see me now!

The format of BL's routine sometimes resulted in friction between BL and Lou DiVito, who resented having to stop the flow of music to play BL's signature songs. The tension was heightened by BL's tendency to be late for his 12:00AM set. As a result, an already frustrated Lou would grow increasingly annoyed, and BL would get flustered and start to cry. To avoid such drama, the staff frequently hustled BL up the stairs behind the stage to make sure he stepped through the mirrored door precisely on time. He was worth the hassle. BL was one of the reasons why the Bistro had become the hottest club in town.

From a 1974 *Chicago Sun Times* piece on the first anniversary of the Bistro: "...a sturdy figure wrapped in a white coat resembling tablecloth damask came out, green lights flashing under the coat at chest level, illuminating its pattern. Rows of ruffles jiggled under the coat's hem, revealing high platform shoes.
"At first one saw only his back, but at last the figure danced a half turn to reveal – behind a turquoise feather fan and white plastic rimmed dark glasses – the Bearded Lady. As eager fans handed up folding money, he took off layers down to a Carmen Miranda dress over a bra."

Sometimes BL took a microphone on stage and, following his performance, began a stream of consciousness monologue. "Lots of really good people here tonight. I'm the Bearded Lady and this is the Bistro." BL could be witty, but he needed a foil. His best impromptu chats included barbs with DJ Lou, who would retort on his microphone from the booth. The crowd ate it up. When Lou grew tired of listening to BL, he would simply cut BL's microphone and turn up the music.

During his Bistro days, BL compulsively scoured resale and thrift shops for new outfits. Though he proclaimed himself the Queen of AmVets, he enjoyed junking at other thrift stores as well. He enjoyed the resale shops lining Lincoln Avenue, the resale shops south on Halsted, and those along 32nd and 33rd in Bridgeport. Friends like Carol Cheeseman, Jimmy Blythe, and Peter Bellinder often accompanied him on his shopping sprees.

To see BL in any retail environment was to see him in his element. He was always talking and flirting. He would pick up this and that, often something colorful, sparkly, or strange; and begin wondering aloud, "What can I do with that? How can I make that into something? What if I bought a dozen of these?" BL could be very crafty. Anything and everything had outfit potential.

BL delighted in closing the Bistro on a Saturday night, removing some of his hair props, hopping in a cab with a couple friends, and heading for Maxwell Street on Chicago's near South Side. At the multi-ethnic bazaar, vendors were already set up over several square blocks for the Sunday morning shoppers. Maxwell Street was ideal for BL. He found oodles of costume jewelry as well as styles of clothing from different eras and other cultures. Best of all, the Maxwell Street prices were cheap and negotiable. After a couple of hours his friends would be ready for bed but, powered by a night's worth of cocaine, BL would continue shopping.

Since he was buying so much jewelry, BL soon developed a keen eye for the quality, authenticity, and craftsmanship of each piece. As with most things he collected, he became a self-educated expert on broaches, earrings, and necklaces. BL loathed buying anything fake or poorly crafted. The thought of being ripped off made him physically ill.

Although he wasn't choosy about the clothes he wore at the Bistro, BL began to study fashion. He made a weekly pilgrimage to Rizzoli bookstore in Water Tower Place to buy every fashion magazine in stock: *W*, *Vogue*, *Women's Wear Daily*, *Cosmopolitan*, *Elle*, etc. At Fiorucci he'd buy all the Euro fashion magazines that Rizzoli didn't stock; paying from the rubber-banded wad of cash he kept in a snakeskin purse.

Prior to becoming a disco, the basement of the Bistro had been a storage area and changing room for restaurant staff. In the dingy dressing room, with assorted lockers, tables, and mirrors, BL kept piles and garbage bags of garments and frocks, accessories, and props. Since this was a communal area for all Bistro performers, some coworkers became upset with him for having his clothes strewn everywhere. Every night BL rummaged through the piles to put something together. If a garment didn't quite fit, BL got a pair of scissors and made it fit. He had enough clothes to fill a couple of warehouses.

Sometimes adding to his extensive wardrobe caused offense. When a friend's mother died, BL called and asked, "What are you going to do with all her old clothes?"

In addition to the Bistro's basement, BL's wardrobe dominated his own apartment. For years, he lived in a studio on Briar between Broadway and Sheridan. Friends picking him up for work or play were rarely allowed inside. (BL may have been worried they wouldn't fit.) He was what many might label "a hoarder." His apartment had pathways to walk through, with clutter and boxes and clothing piled floor to ceiling in areas. After living there a few years, BL's landlord caught a glimpse of the inside of the apartment and promptly evicted him.

BL moved to a larger apartment in a brick six-flat at 4408 N. Dover where "a forest of clothing racks" held the brunt of his massive wardrobe. His acquisitions dominated every square inch of his new place as well.

Clothes remained a necessity for him. Although the Bistro, Chicago nightlife, and the LGBT community had evolved, BL's act remained relatively the same: *Love's Theme*, *Who's That Lady*, a current hit, hand fans, sunglasses, and layers of clothing. The consistency didn't hurt his popularity. In fact, his fame only seemed to increase. In a slight nod to change, BL would sometimes have a go-go boy or two behind him.

Sometimes he made exceptions. When he performed *Honeybee* by Gloria Gaynor he came to the stage *through* the bar instead of from the back of the mirrored stage. Imagine a somewhat high-pitched voice leading an entourage. *"Coming through please.*

Coming through please." Then there was BL… in a gold lamé beekeeper outfit (including the netting), with a feathered hand fan, and a headdress resembling immense insect antennae. Trailing along in his wake were drones – young "gay-bees" in yellow and black carrying hatboxes and flowers, lampshades, and robes. The message was clear: BL was Queen of the Hive.

That's Where the Happy People Go

Less than a year after the Bistro opened, on April 7, 1974, writer Lynn Van Matre wrote in the *Chicago Tribune* piece "Secure sexuality . . . and the scene sells:

> "Once upon a time, the Bistro was a restaurant . . . * * * The French fare, and the restaurant itself, vanished from the scene more than a year ago, replaced by a scene. Lighted neon lips glow on the walls, the music starts at 10, and the dancing doesn't stop 'til 4 – either on the discotheque floor or above, where a couple of male dancers, including a Bearded Lady decked out in dowdy drag for comic relief, ply their trade by turns. The Bistro, or Dugan's Bistro as the bar and disco answers to these days, is unabashedly gay. It is also the essence of hipness.
>
> "And in case you haven't noticed, the two have become synonymous to a certain degree. * * * Not that gay, of course, has always been synonymous with good. Up until a few years ago, gay meant hassles, as the owners and patrons of earlier gay bars well know. "I opened at a great time," says Edward [Dugan] Davison, a very together 28, who lent his name to Dugan's Bistro and spends 18 hours a day running the place.
>
> "For the last two years, there's been a very cool atmosphere as far as the law goes." * * * Now the gay scene pays off another way, in terms of American capitalism. The Bistro does good business – just try to get in on a Saturday night around midnight, when the lines have

been known to stretch a block back to Clark Street."

On the black asphalt and vinyl dance floor of the Bistro, celebrities rubbed elbows with the LGBT community, and edgy discophiles. A number of patrons were eager to add to the frenetic atmosphere, especially if their ability to shock got them got through the door faster. From the *Chicago Tribune* piece, *Swinging at Dugan's Bistro*, by Jon Anderson, "...it brought together people who looked like go-go boys, construction workers, Indian princesses, vampires, prom queens, and Bette Davis."

Sometimes partygoers at the Bistro even encountered straight people from the suburbs. As its popularity soared, the Bistro became one of the first venues in the city where gay people mixed and partied with straights in a friendly atmosphere. As *Chicago Magazine* once wrote, "Sooner or later, everyone ends up at the Bistro."

The Bistro was selective about admittance. Not everyone made it beyond the glitter-strewn sidewalk. Even if the club was below their 500 person capacity, Eddie considered it good business to have a line at the door. On weekends, the queue to get inside was sometimes two blocks long. Eddie liked that feeling of selectivity, and picking people that fit the bar's "image." Anticipation heightened the experience. Later, Steve Rubell at Studio 54 adopted a similar door policy.

Being young, cute, "interesting," or shirtless helped patrons get in the door faster, but there were no guarantees. Once inside, being hot might mean lots of attention, free drinks, or offers of drugs. The only rule for those who made it over the threshold was to leave your hang-ups at the door. "Negative vibes" were not tolerated at the Bistro.

When it came to door policy, Eddie was adamant that heterosexuals would never be the norm at the Bistro. He made it emphatically clear to every doorman on their first night of work that the Bistro was primarily a gay club, and he intended on keeping it that way. He wanted outrageousness, fabulousness, and sexy, sweaty, bare-chested guys on the dance floor. He wanted same-sex grinding and the hint of homo-sex in the air. Eddie was unshakable in resolve to protect the gay vibe.

When asked in a 1974 piece by the *Chicago Tribune* about the Bistro's restrictive door policies, Dugan replied, "We're primarily gay, and we don't want straights filling the place up so our regular clientele can't get in." Eddie had no problem letting straight people into the bar, in moderation. Eddie was always aware of the ratio. The balance of the crowd was key to him.

Despite the clamor and demand that came with the surge of the discotheque's popularity, and the prices he could have charged, Eddie never wavered on his stance. If people wanted a straight disco, with men in leisure suits and gold chains and the women in Halston dresses, they were welcome to go to Faces on Rush or BBC aka the Bombay Bicycle Club on Division.

Nights when the Bistro teetered on the brink of being too straight, Eddie encouraged flamboyant and raunchy dancing among the gay patrons. Eddie liked to "scandalize the straights," who wanted to experience the "wildness" of a big city club. More than a few in the community were eager to sex up the dance floor, and give those *heteros* something to watch. The Bearded Lady was always willing to comply. Both on stage and off stage, BL enjoyed propositioning, embarrassing, and sometimes even scoring, with straight men.

There was no mistaking the double standard at the Bistro. One evening a straight couple started fucking in the larger stall in the women's bathroom. The two were oblivious to polite knocks. Rather than let it go, a couple staff members got on a chair and dumped a bucket of ice water over the top of the cubicle onto the twosome. The soaked couple shrieked and fled out the side door. To make things worse, it was the middle of winter.

In a 1974 interview, Eddie voiced his surprise at how being gay has "caught on": "It sort of puzzles me because gay people usually like to be left alone, and suddenly the whole scene's become fashionable." Overnight it seemed as though things were changing. In some circles, being gay had become the essence of hipness.

Fashionable or not, Eddie made certain the scene was never boring. To emphasize the "anything can happen" vibe at the Bistro, Eddie was known to encourage drag dancers to get up on the main oval bar and kick every single thing off the counter and onto the floor: drinks, bar napkins, ashtrays, cigarettes, everything went flying. Glasses smashed on the tile. Afterwards, Eddie had the bartender replace everything and gave those at the bar a free round of drinks. Eddie knew people would repeat the story about "the crazy thing" that happened at the Bistro last night. He considered it the best kind of advertising.

Having interesting regulars was another kind of publicity and at the Bistro there were plenty of them. There was Regina, a dominatrix who typically arrived with her submissive husband on a leash, a woman who wore an outfit made of chains, the diapered Disco Baby, the vampire couple, and a music lover who was fond of dancing with a 33 1/3 LP record affixed in his hair.

Regulars "Jane" and "Liz" were the Turquoise Girls, or the Sparkle Girls, or the Tasty Twins… everyone seemed to have a different name for them; but everyone knew who they were: two straight women who dyed their hair the same blonde shade, styled it the same, dressed in identical outfits every night, and usually danced together.

The professional gay song and dance group, the Cycle Sluts, whom *the Hollywood Reporter* called "banned, barred, and X-rated," stopped by the Bistro whenever they were in town. The dozen or so members (with names like Gloria Hole and Lola Loin) arrived in full make-up and leather gear. Most members were seven feet tall with teased hair and heels. Members of the macho-drag group snaked in a single-file line through the Bistro before making their way out and heading to the next bar. This free form of promotion let every gay person in the River North area that night know the Cycle Sluts were performing in town. Eddie liked the theatrics of it all. The appearance of the Cycle Sluts was something else people would talk about.

The Bistro was one of the few places a fashion forward heiress and successful Chicago businesswoman felt comfortable enough to repeatedly shout, "Humiliate Me!" in public. Random eccentric behavior contributed to the uncontrollable lunacy of the place.

Recording much of the action was photographer Al Carter. Al took photos of people with a Polaroid camera, inserted the picture into a cardboard sleeve, and sold them for $5. Al was a pro, often holding a flashlight between his knees or beneath his chin, to light the shot perfectly. Al's tool belt was his travelling office with pens, stapler, photo sleeves, and extra Polaroid film.

However, one of the biggest draws at the Bistro was Eddie himself. One Saturday night, Eddie rode a motorcycle about the interior of the Bistro, zipping around the perimeter of the dance floor to a cheering drunken crowd. Another night, he instigated a fire extinguisher fight with an employee. The two men ran around the club; downstairs, upstairs, across the dance floor, spraying each other with flame retardant, and emptying the canisters of every bit of foam.

Eddie's birthdays were always something to behold. His 1980 birthday party had a Roman Orgy theme, but the bash was more than a typical toga party. Eddie had the entire four bartender/four drink station of the front bar covered with plywood. Fountains and greenery were added for "atmosphere." In the lush setting, Eddie reclined on oversized pillows and had gorgeous young men in G-strings fan him with palms and feed him grapes. He also had a hole drilled in the ceiling above the dance floor. At midnight he descended through the opening and into a bathtub. Once he was lowered, a group of scantily clad young men stepped forward and filled the tub with champagne.

Eddie's birthday the following year had a circus theme. For the event wild caged animals were brought into the bar. When the man arrived with the animals, he discovered the lion cage was too big to fit through the door. Eddie decided to let the lion out, and have the cage disassembled and reassembled inside. While the task with the enclosure took place, the lion was tethered in the bar and eventually "rounded up" to get back into his cage. At midnight, Eddie swung from the ceiling on a trapeze. At the same party, TL emerged from the ceiling hole in the palm of King Kong's hand to perform a production number.

Another year his birthday theme was gangsters and flappers with the Bistro transformed into a speakeasy. Patrons, who wanted to jump the line wore pinstriped suits, fringed dresses with long strings of beads, carried tommy guns, and flashed hip flasks. The password to get inside was "Dugan."

Eddie's birthdays were always a spectacle with free drinks and cavorting galore. One or two or even more naked guys usually jumped out of the cake and most shirtless boys in the club ended up covered in cake frosting.

His parents, Edward Sr. and Helen, were usually in attendance at his parties. The Davison's put up with a lot from their son and knew what was going on with the drugs and whatnot, but their love and support of Eddie was unconditional. Eddie worshipped his parents. He was frequently concerned about where they were going to be seated at special Bistro gatherings and how to make them more comfortable. He usually didn't invite them to the post-party get-togethers upstairs.

The loft apartment upstairs was popular for the hush-hush after hours Bistro parties where the drugs, alcohol, and nudity were even more plentiful. More than once Eddie was known to appear in drag at these bashes as Vicki Edie. The Bistro private parties were legendary, and Eddie knew the power of legends.

At one of the parties, approximately sixty people were in attendance when there was a raid. Forty-five people escaped down some back stairs and scattered into the streets. The remaining fifteen partygoers were arrested. Some attendees were too wasted to move. Several over-indulgers had to be carried to the paddy wagon. At the station Eddie approached the desk with enough cash in his pocket to pay everyone's bail. The right legal representation made the incident "go away."

Holiday decorations at the Bistro were something else people talked about, something "you have to see." Eddie had done windows for upscale retailers in New York City prior to immersing himself in Chicago's bar world. He brought his deep love for over-the-top yuletide decor to the Bistro and spent thousands on decorations.

During the holidays, the Bistro featured mountains of assorted wrapped presents, Christmas trees laden with ornaments, automated elves, Santa Claus, reindeer, suspended sleighs, snowflakes, tinsel, and holiday lights by the hundreds. One year the Bistro had a decorated tree hung upside down, blinking lights and all. Beside the tree were upside down gifts, an upside down rocking chair, and an upside down Santa and reindeer. Each year the Bistro's decor grew more extravagant. Seeing and being a part of that became a tradition for many people. The Bistro staff holiday party featured Christmas trees laden with assorted (and some illegal) "party favors."

Eddie's philosophy was, "When you give back to people, they'll keep giving to you."

More, More, More

As befitting the era, the Bearded Lady was a person of enormous appetites: drugs, disco, sex, and food. He could eat dozens of egg rolls in one sitting, loved fried rice, and drank gallons of chocolate milk. BL enjoyed going to new restaurants and sampling different cuisines.

Sexually, he seemed insatiable. He tricked a lot and slept little. Lust was part of his persona. He was described as, "the most flirtatious go-go boy ever, but in a round man's body and wearing a dress." Attracted to men with facial hair, BL would sometimes catch a hunk's eye from the stage and challenge them to a strip off. Since BL wore multiple layers, he always won. Lusty and aggressive, BL was never shy about sex. He was notorious for having busy and groping hands.

In Sukie de la Croix's Chicago Whispers section of *the Windy City Times*, Nick S. said, "We didn't really like each other. I just didn't like him, and he didn't like me. He was really big at the Bistro and my lover and I used to go there a lot, and he knew my lover. I remember one night we were there and he came up and started talking with my lover, and fondling him and stuff, and I was really pissed off. I pushed her away, and she said, 'Do you know who I am?' and I said, 'I don't care who you are, this is my lover and you don't touch him if I'm around.'"

BL was fond of grabbing hot guys from the audience to join him on stage during his third number. Oftentimes those men were led, sometimes lured, through the mirrored door on the back of the stage, down the backstage stairs, to the right, and down to the dressing room in the basement. BL was extremely generous with his expert blowjobs. At the Bistro he was interrupted blowing guys in the bathroom and the coat check. Sometimes, his hand fan concealed droplets of semen in his beard.

One night, BL was due on stage for his 2:00AM set, but was nowhere to be found. He was eventually discovered in the basement, amongst the piles of clothes, getting fucked over an ironing board. Rather than be embarrassed, BL said he'd be there in a minute. "That was so *so* good," He later said, with a flutter of his hand fan and mock fluster of "Oh! *Oh!*"

Cruising for sex amongst the bushes adjacent to the Lincoln Park Lagoon, a popular spot for hot gay action, was one of BL's favorite pastimes. He also liked tricking near the small embankment by the North Pond in Lincoln Park, referred to at the time as "Sissy Hill." BL was never embarrassed about sex. He brought lightheartedness and a sense of fun to being promiscuous.

During this sexually active period, BL also had boyfriends. For six years (1974-1980) he dated Billy G., a slender man with a glass eye he sometimes removed to entertain people. The relationship was fraught with drama. BL had a weakness for intense men, especially ones with facial hair.

BL dated Jack F. from 1980-1982. Like most gay relationships of the era, BL's were open. He had a boyfriend and enjoyed the pleasures of other men as well. He was a prime example of the revolutionary attitudes towards sex that followed the gay liberation movement. There was no conflict. Possessiveness was taboo. Sexual liberation was all about having the option to be as free as a person wanted to be. Few in the LGBT community wanted to ape the "unnatural" hetero style of monogamy.

BL was having an enormous amount of fun with his life and his fame. Star fuckers were welcome. BL was recognized anywhere and everywhere. In the River North area, BL could drink for free in most of the dozen or so gay bars nearby. One of his favorite haunts was the Gold Coast. BL was drawn to the sexy energy of leather bars, but rarely wore leather. Instead, he typically wore a caftan or ecclesiastic robes. This included a headdress. Doormen in the area recall seeing BL exiting taxis head first to avoid damaging his elaborate headgear.

At times, BL's ego interfered, causing friction with Eddie who grew so irked at one point that he had the phrase "Home of the Bearded Lady" removed from the Bistro sign. Eddie claimed that BL had become impossible. "She thinks she's Elizabeth Taylor, demanding a private dressing room, caviar on her dressing table, and 24-hour limousine service. I'm already giving her all the champagne she can drink."

The Bistro "family," especially the performers, were rife with strong personalities and several big but fragile egos. The backstage Bistro environment could sometimes be very catty, often competitive, and frequently cliquish. Drama was an ongoing reality. Sometimes feuds were even encouraged.

Several employees resented BL's star trip. Others claim there was no bad attitude and that the root of the problem sprang from jealousy over the attention BL was receiving. By the start of 1975, things had rapidly deteriorated. Words were said. People felt betrayed. Drugs fuelled much of the drama. In the spring of 1975, BL got into an enormous fight with one of the managers and quit. For months he performed at private parties and occasionally at other venues.

During the 1975 Gay Pride Parade, BL was marching with another bar. As fate would have it, the Bistro float was directly behind them. Egged on by staff members, Danny "Dee Dee" Celebron (in a sparkly top and emerald green skirt, leotards, and green heels) leapt from the Bistro float and dumped a full cooler of ice water on top of BL's plumed headdress right in the middle of Clark and Diversey. BL was promptly escorted from the scene.

Eventually, differences between BL and the Bistro staff were resolved. He returned to the club after his "hiatus." At the Bistro BL was a star, and he liked being in the limelight.

Stardom prompted him to start using the name Bobby Starr, sometimes with one "r" and sometimes with two. "When you're a star it doesn't matter," he joked. BL thought of Bobby Starr (or Star) as his semi-stage name. He was Bobby Starr, "The Bearded Lady." On stage he was the Bearded Lady. Offstage, but still in the public eye, he was Bobby Starr. In Chicago, BL never used Bob Theiss in connection with his performance work. His real name was reserved for those who knew him apart from the glitz and glitter, like close friends and family. To tricks, if he used a name at all, it was Bob Starr as well.

In those days, BL's favorite topic was cock. He loved to gossip about Bistro co-workers and customers. He found it delicious to discuss who had slept with whom, the size of their endowment, and what they preferred sexually. He wasn't unique. Many Bistro staffers were obsessed with juicy carnal details. BL absorbed the piquant buzz and expounded upon what he heard with racy bits. In other words, he was an accomplished gossipmonger.

BL could be tough to get off the telephone. He often made calls from his phone beside the kitchen sink with his two cockatiels squawking in the background. His talk was often of his sexual exploits, with the intimate details of each trick: size, shape, position, etc. When a friend finally said, "Enough...BL where do you stop?" BL responded, "Usually at the base." Some people wondered what words those birds eventually learned.

He liked having birds and fish as pets because he felt they were able to appreciate being taken care of while remaining behind bars or glass. Fish could even be decorative. Two of BL's most popular accessories, as reported in the columns, were his clear Lucite platform shoes with a live goldfish swimming in the heels. BL debuted the newsworthy accessory in 1978 in a performance of the Voyage song *Souvenirs*. For the number, he wore a silk and lace dress and twirled a matching parasol. To showcase the shoes, he had two young men on hands and knees licking his heels.

Common BL sayings included "Statements have been made" and "In your face." If BL was discussing a trick he sometimes described that person as being "in my face, in a gracious way." A statement that also hinted at his love of oral sex. Sometimes BL called himself Mama, a reference to Mama Rose in *Gypsy*: "Mama's going to make sure he doesn't do that." "Mama has an itch that needs scratching." He often adopted this tone when talking with young people new to the LGBT community.

A cassette tape exists of BL and some friends at a 1979 holiday celebration. On the recording, BL is immediately recognizable. His rapid chatter is interspersed by excited screams and squeals.

More than anything he actually *says*, BL's larger than life personality emerges in his loud, infectious, and very theatrical laugh. His laughter is reminiscent of a bygone era. At various times his chuckle resembles that of Jonathan Winters, Charles Nelson Reilly, and/or Phyllis Diller. His laughter was a complex and layered language.

BL giggled and talked, a lot. His natural tendency for loquaciousness ran amok under the influence of cocaine. He was extremely social. Friends joked that he rarely stopped talking. Despite his obvious intelligence and apparent expertise on numerous subjects, he was rarely serious.

An exception was when Robert Sr. died of leukemia on September 30, 1980 in Clearwater, FL. His mother, Kay, did not want BL to go to his father's funeral. BL told friends that she was angry with him. Kay wanted her son to get married and have children. Kay was as stubborn as her son. BL went to the funeral anyway. Although the situation was tense, he was grateful that he went. Attending the services gave him closure. BL was saying goodbye to his father as well as something more. The funeral helped BL to accept that he was never going to be the son his parents wanted him to be.

Funkytown

In the early days of gay liberation, the bars were the most visible businesses in the community. The taverns and clubs were hubs of activity. Bars were where gay people congregated, spent money, and had fun. By coming together the community recognized its scope and power, so it's not surprising that the bars were frequently the seats of political activity, and often located near each other.

As the 1970s progressed, the Bistro became more politically involved. In October 1978, the Bistro hosted Leonard Matlovich (decorated Vietnam vet who "outed" himself to fight the ban on gays in the military), Reverend Troy Perry (founder of the Metropolitan Community Church) and Dave Kopay (former NFL running back who came out as gay in 1975) as special guests at the Harvest Table for Human Rights. The benefit and art auction was sponsored by Illinoisans to Stop the Briggs Initiative aka Proposition 6, a proposed conservative measure that would have banned lesbians and gays from working in California schools.

In February of 1979 the Bistro threw a party for Washington's Birthday. The benefit auction was organized by Eddie Dugan and Chuck Renslow for Alderman Clifford Kelly, a force in local politics and the man billed as the Father of Chicago's original Gay Rights Bill. Though the event was political, it was still given a Bistro spin. Ads for the fundraiser featured George Washington with sexy revelers. Above the ad, the copy read, "I cannot tell a lie...it's gonna be a HOT PARTY!!"

Despite his political involvement, Eddie saw the Bistro's main function as being a place to party. Eddie believed that the party was the reason for it all and that the objective of everything was to have fun. Given this outlook on life and the world, Eddie always found a way to turn something bad into something good. This included renovations.

The Bistro was a work in progress. Slight alterations in décor were happening to some degree most of the time. There were two major overhauls. The first was in 1975. The second, in 1979, was a massive renovation that required closing for six-weeks. The latter remodeling session took place during a penalty period when Dugan's liquor license had been suspended following an after-hours party.

When faced with the censure and a pending decor overhaul, Eddie approached the situation in the same manner he did almost everything, he turned it into a party. On the eve of the closure, the Bistro had a Demolition Party. Ropes, hardhats, and a wheelbarrow of sledgehammers were placed in various areas throughout the bar. Dugan then instructed the staff to let patrons smash the designated portions of the interior.

On the night of the Demolition Party, Eddie had an added surprise. Pulling TL aside, he told him that when BL went through the door and onto the stage, TL was to lock the door behind him. TL didn't know what Eddie had in mind, but it was apparent by the look on his face that it was going to be fun.

That night when BL finished his set, TL and Eddie stepped forward with sledgehammers and began to smash the corners of the stage. Unable to flee through the locked stage door, BL yelped and shouted, "Oh! Oh! *Oh!*" More of the stage broke apart and the remaining platform tilted forward. BL shrieked for Eddie to stop, but the screams of the crowd were louder than his pleas. Eventually Eddie put down his sledgehammer and shouted that drinks were on the house.

One area marked for destruction was the wall on the upper floor that separated the dance floor area from the back seating room. The compliant and inebriated crowd took the sledgehammers and demolished the wall that night, making the two rooms into one. With the room opened up, the revamped dance floor eventually assumed a different shape.

Following the demolition, the tables and chairs in the seating area were taken to the basement. A curved three-station bar, the "Boogie Bar," was installed in the back corner. On one side were three banquettes and on the other side was Planet Janet's VIP lounge area with the five banquettes.

The built-in benches brought cohesiveness to the Bistro, uniting the look of the oval bar area on the first floor and the renovated back bar space. Additional cohesiveness came from the fresh flowers behind both front and back bars. Eddie delighted in going to the flower market and placing his orders. The floral arrangements were sometimes three feet high and three feet wide. Smaller "accent" arrangements adorned the ledges between the booths.

Holidays were always a fine reason for celebration. The Bistro had enormous Valentine's Day bashes, Spring Fever parties, Bicentennial Parties (*Red, White and Blue attire! A table of wine and cheese!*), Friday the 13th parties (*Get Lucky!*), April Fool's Day parties (Tiny Tim was the surprise guest in 1979), Polynesian-themed parties, and blow-outs for almost every holiday. Easter meant Easter baskets, a bonnet contest, and hardboiled eggs at the bar. Halloween parties were spectacular and included a staff theme such as Ancient Egypt, Mortuary Madness, Safari, Drag, and the Very Wild West.

The 1977 Halloween shindig was billed as the "War of the Stars." Prizes were given for Best Space Costume, Best General Costume, and Best Drag Costume. Special Bistro touches for this particular party included "a trip to the Inter-galactic Disco and Star Wars Lounge" and an area designated as "the Planet of the Giant Spiders."

In 1976, The Bistro was featured in the film *Looking for Mr. Goodbar*. Eddie and some Bistro employees can be glimpsed in the early crowd scenes and walking along Rush Street. In the movie, Eddie and his then boyfriend are seen holding hands, something deemed quite risqué at the time. Both men are wearing their own fur coats. Director Richard Brooks wanted to populate his movie with "colorful" characters. Featuring Eddie in the film was the trade off for allowing some of the disco scenes to be shot at the Bistro. The club also hosted the wrap party with a guest list that included Diane Keaton, Tom Berenger, Tuesday Weld, and movie newcomer Richard Gere.

In 1978 Chicago bar legend Medusa had a theme party at the Bistro. An ad for the affair read: "This anti-chic gala is scheduled to start at 10 p.m. with a dress [code] theme that's being billed as sleazy, lowdown, fuckpig... The door charge will include a complimentary bottle of poppers, a free buffet, plus many unmentionable surprises." Follow-up for the event was covered by Richard Cooke in *Gay Chicago*, "Medusa Ann Wallflower also held her biggie at Dugan's Bistrotheque last Friday night. The party titled 'Medusa Pigs Out at the Bistro' gave Chicago gays the chance to really sleaze it up. Some of the things that stuck out included over 1,000 White Castle Hamburgers that were royally passed out to guests on silver trays, and [a] hundred sticks of incense that were lighted and handed out to the appreciating crowd. I recalled seeing a dead baby pig on a buffet table, an old soiled mattress in the middle of the dance floor, and an ironing board in Janet Johnson's [the Planet] lounge area!"

Eddie always craved a crowd. He didn't like to arrive much before midnight and when he did he wanted the party to be in full swing. Given the number of gay nightspots nearby, it was sometimes challenging to drum up business on slower nights of the week. To boost numbers, the Bistro tried anything and everything from couples disco dance contests to wet jockey short contests. Wet shorts contests became a regular Wednesday night event hosted by flamboyant emcee Deluxe. The theme song of the evening was a parody of a popular ABBA song, *The Weiner Takes It All*.

The Bistro had nights where men in dago-tees got in free. Other nights, bare-chested men got through the door without a cover. On "Cinderella Special Fridays" the cover was a dollar until midnight. The Bistro had fashion shows, cast parties, raffles, U.S.O. talent shows, and the popular Mr. Bistro contests. On record giveaway nights, Lou passed out numerous promotional discs to the appreciative crowd.

The Bistro also hosted photography exhibits and art shows, like the showing by popular Chicago artist of the era Jon Reich [1953-

1992], nationally recognized as a leading gay talent. Reich's flashy clothes also earned him the nickname, "The Liberace of the Arts."

Sundays were movie nights. The Bistro showed everything from Lana Turner in *Madame X* to a Mae West double feature to Mel Brooks' *The Producers*. During the six-week closure in 1979 for renovations, the Gold Coast took over movie nights on Sunday. Showing films at the bars was popular in the pre-video era. By the end of the summer Carol's Speakeasy hosted a movie night on Tuesdays. The Glory Hole and Broadway Limited had movie nights as well. After the 1979 reopening, the Bistro stopped having movie night and instead started "Super Summer Sundays," giving away two ten-speed bikes every week and serving complimentary champagne at midnight.

On Mondays, Eddie and the crew hoped a revue/variety show would bring in a crowd. In early 1979, *GayLife* columnist Richard Cooke wrote, "Janet Johnson, 'The First Lady of the Bistro' was back on stage again last Monday for the *Show of Shows*. The only word that describes Janet is madcap... Janet and Ethel are the Bistro's two most popular ladies."

[Cooke's closing remark was referring to the popular VIP-area waitress as well as the popularity of ethyl chloride as a party drug. Ethyl chloride was something Eddie "discovered" in New York. He enjoyed it so much he bought a case and brought it back to Chicago.]

Monday night's *Show of Shows* happened at midnight. The popular revue showcased top drag performers. In 1979 *Gay Chicago* teased, "*The Monday Show of Shows* will be returning to Dugan's Bistrotheque this fall with the TL Noble Revue heading up the first night of zany entertainment... This year's shows promises to be exciting with several new female impersonators from out of the state, a magician, puppeteer Steve Margrave (who has gained a reputation second only, perhaps, to Wayland Flowers)... psychic Annie Rose, plus local Chicago personalities, which will include Chicago Molly, Bertha Butt, Chilli Pepper, Rita, the Shopping Bag Lady. And, after two years of seclusion, Audrey Bryant, also will be joining the popular Monday night activities..."

Comedians were also booked at the Bistro. Insult comic Beverly "Pudgy" Wines (who went to high school with Eddie) performed there. The extremely popular standup comic was often compared to Joan Rivers and Totie Fields. Pudgy worked at Punchinello's, emceed the International Mr. Leather contest, and appeared several times at the Bistro. Wayland Flowers and his lusty octogenarian puppet, Madame, were also a hit with the Bistro crowd as was popular comedic impressionist Alan Lozito. Sometimes referred to as the Man of a Thousand Faces – and one of Eddie's favorite comics – Lozito was booked several times at the club.

Drag performers also brought in business. Dina Jacobs, Roski Fernandez, Lilly White, Joanne Caron (Empress of Chicago, 1980), Chanel Dupree, Kitty Litter, Terri Page (*the Pantomime Rage!*), Heather Fontaine, Junie Moon, Artesia Wells, Sherri Payne, Ginger Grant, Lisa Eaton, Latese Chevron, Diana Hutton, Jody Lee, Leslie Rejeanne, Choo Choo La Fanne, and Wanda Lust all sparkled on the Bistro stage.

Thursdays at the Bistro was a two-dollar cover with all drinks, except for call brands, 75 cents! Thursdays often featured some sloppy entertainment off the stage. If drink specials were the way to get people to the Bistro on off-nights, Eddie was happy to oblige. To get people going out in the middle of the week during the winter months, Eddie eventually had a "Winter Get Ya Out Sale" – all Drinks 50 cents, call brands a dollar, Monday through Friday.

At the Bistro, many on staff were partying just as heavily as the clientele, often indulging before work, during work, and after work. Many not only worked together, but also partied together, and slept together as well. Most staffers referred to themselves as part of the "Bistro Family." For some, these "chosen family" relationships were crucial. Biological families often rejected their LGBT kids, either outright or by not making an effort to understand them. The bond shared by many coworkers was one of the things that made the Bistro magical.

Eddie fostered staunch loyalty among his staff. His praise meant a great deal. Though he could be demanding, he treated his workers like an integral part of his ongoing party. Bartenders, doormen, wait staff, and entertainers all felt like they were making this great thing happen together – and they were.

In the Bistro surrogate/dysfunctional family, Eddie was the head of the brood. Though he was the provider, he was not necessarily a parental figure. Eddie more closely resembled "Auntie" Mame Dennis, whom often quoted: "Life is a banquet, and most poor sons-of-bitches are starving to death!"

Staff parties were wild and excessive. The booze flowed freely and Eddie provided the drugs. They were typically slated to end at midnight with the bar opening afterwards. But the revelry often got out of hand and soon Eddie – and the staff – might be too distracted to remember the time, or be too wasted to walk, much less work, by midnight.

At the end of the New Year's Eve shift at 5:00AM, Eddie had two large busses parked outside, ready to whisk the staff and their guests (lovers/tricks/etc.) to Nutbush City Limits in Forest Park so they could enjoy their own party. The busses were loaded with bottles of champagne, as well as cocaine, joints, and poppers. By the time the busses hissed to a stop the staff was feeling no pain. As with all employee outings, Eddie picked up the tab for everything.

Some nights after closing, Eddie continued partying with employees and friends at his modern 2-bedroom 2-bath apartment on the 29th floor of the East Tower of a high rise at 345 W. Fullerton. Décor touches in Eddie's deco place included silver blinds, deep purple walls, and parquet floors. The blinds at Eddie's place were heavy to keep out the daylight and keep the party atmosphere going strong. If anyone parted the blinds, even a bit, they were resoundingly booed. Sunshine ruined the buzz. Daylight was always a threat to the ongoing party. Eddie's get-togethers routinely featured an assortment of half-naked young men. BL was often there. He adored nudity

Eddie took good care of those in his inner circle. Several Bistro folks, including Lou DiVito, lived in the same building. TL Noble lived in Eddie's second bedroom. Not surprisingly, Eddie paid the rent for them both.

Eddie's non-stop revelry sometimes resulted in problems. Bistro lawyer Ron Ehemann is quoted in *Leatherman: The Legend of Chuck Renslow* as saying, "Eddie had 'disappearing issues' – he'd be gone for a week and no one would have any idea where he went." Any night Eddie might empty a cash register and take off. Once, he disappeared for an entire month in Hawaii. The reasons behind his extended absences were typically a drug and alcohol bender, a love affair, or some combination of the two.

After graduating from law school in the late 1970s, Ron Ehemann penned the *Speaking Of* column in *GayLife* newspaper. One day Eddie called and asked, "I just have one question for you, are you really gay?" When Ron said he was, Eddie hired him. The next morning Eddie arrived at Ron's office with Lou and TL in tow. Eddie was dragging a full-length fox coat, still out from the night before.

In no time, Ehemann was working out of Eddie's private Bistro office three nights a week. Ron didn't represent the Bistro the entire time, but Eddie offered him use of his office for meeting with clients. Ron represented a lot of night people and meeting at the Bistro during bar hours was convenient for everyone. The Bistro also had a good amount of legal problems. Usually it was drugs, door policy, or after-hours parties that caused the issues and lawsuits. Sometimes the charges were different.

In June of 1973, after being open only seventeen days, a lawsuit was filed, charging that the Bistro knowingly permitted "lewd conduct and fondling by patrons." Police offers witnessed two men in a booth, "kissing each other and fondling each other in and around the groin. The conduct continued off and on for approximately 10-15 minutes." The two men, and Eddie, were arrested. Charges were dismissed at a hearing.

In 1974, a Bistro doorman was accused of battery, but the circumstances were hazy, the witnesses were drunk, as was the supposed victim of the assault. Around the same time, charges were filed citing another doorman who denied a patron entry without a lawful reason, supposedly for being female. A lawsuit regarding discriminatory carding was filed in 1977. Several cases challenged the bar's posted door policy requiring five forms of I.D.

Some argued it was a way to keep out African-American patrons. Others claimed the policy prevented straights from overrunning the club. Most of those filing charges failed to appear in court. A couple of lawsuits resulted in financial settlements. More than once the charges led to a temporary suspension of the Bistro's liquor license.

Discriminatory door policy was the reason for the picket outside the Bistro on Labor Day weekend of 1980. Over two-dozen protestors marched in front of the disco from midnight until 2:00 AM. The Committee of Black Gay Men organized the demonstration though other groups participated in the picketing.

In response to the protests, Eddie Dugan published a letter in *Gay Chicago*:

> "The Bistro apologizes for any inconvenience or annoyance caused by the appearance of pickets at our door the last two weeks. We don't know exactly why they chose the Bistro but we are so established that small groups have used us before to gain publicity and notoriety. The Bistro was never contacted beforehand but as far as we understand, they are accusing the Bistro of discriminating against Black gay men and gay women.
>
> "The Committee of Black Gay Men is the supposed organization behind the pickets but the two times that they demonstrated only one Black male was in the picket line.
>
> "It is also our understanding that this

committee is an offspring of the R.S.L. (Revolutionary Socialist League) whose flag was prominently displayed in the picket line. The R.S.L. is a known Communist group.

"Our door policy has been the same for seven years. We do not want nor will we ever have an open door policy. Our I.D. policy is to protect you -- our patrons -- from theft and abuse while you are here to party.

"As long as sufficient I.D.'s are presented at the door anyone is welcome at the Bistro.

"Thank you, Edward Dugan."

Eddie refused to let bad news spoil the party. Periodically he would take a wad of cash and call to his entourage, "Let's go to New York." Sometimes he took his posse to Las Vegas or San Francisco. Other times he took them to places like Cleveland. Research was the supposed reason for the excursions. The group was there to experience nightlife, acquire ideas, and keep the Bistro fresh.

Drinks flowed freely and drugs appeared as Eddie and his posse went from nightspot to nightspot. They hit discos, leather bars, sex clubs – the works. Trashed hotel rooms were not uncommon. Curtains were ripped from hallways. Hotel room furniture was completely rearranged, sometimes demolished. Champagne glasses were thrown against walls. Property damage from these "research trips" was often extensive. Eddie picked up the tab, for everything.

Everyone wanted to be in Eddie's inner circle. The entourage was legendary. Eddie and his group burned through millions on drugs and toys and entertainment. In response, Eddie always laughed it off, and would raise his glass in a toast to the lunacy of it all. He could afford it. The Bistro was a phenomenal success. There was money to burn.

Most evenings at the Bistro, the registers were too full of bills to close. Managers made periodic rounds to empty the cash drawers and put the money in the safe. With so much cash, employee skimming was a concern. The Bistro had spies who periodically came to the bar to see if employees were on the take. If someone was caught dipping into the till, they weren't fired. There would be a "conversation" where it was explained that things weren't done that way. No one was ever caught twice.

To guard the cash at the Bistro [for incidentals, bail money, etc.], and to ward off intruders, a Doberman Pinscher named Dugan was released in the bar after closing. Eddie rarely got angry with employees, but he was furious one night when he discovered that someone had given Dugan liquor and the dog was drunk. "When I find out who gave that dog alcohol, they aren't going to be working here anymore." Eddie never found out. One summer night months later, Dugan ran away when someone left the door open. The dog never turned up at any of the city animal rescue centers.

After the dog ran away, the Bistro had a small fire. Someone tossed an ashtray with a smoldering cigarette butt into the coat check garbage. Fortunately, there was only a bit of smoke damage that required some repainting.

The incident made Eddie uneasy. There had been numerous unexplained fires throughout Chicago's gay nightlife scene in the past few years. On May 10, 1975, the Inner Circle – a gay bar and disco that opened with appearances by Andy Warhol and Holly Woodlawn – was gutted by fire. In January of 1976 the Hideaway in Forest Park was damaged by fire. That March, Chuck Renslow's Zolar burned to the ground in a disco inferno. Early Christmas morning in 1977, fire destroyed Le Pub after a mattress started burning in the basement. In 1981 the co-owner of the Haig died of heart failure in his bar while fleeing an explosion and fire suspected of being arson. The Ritz had two suspected arson fires in 1981.

Given the number of "accidental fires," Eddie felt better with someone on the premises at all times. Peter Bellinder was willing so he spent many late nights and early mornings sleeping on one of the gray banquettes after he finished cleaning.

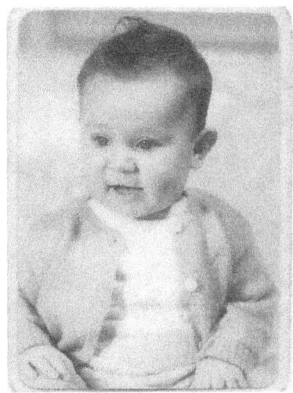
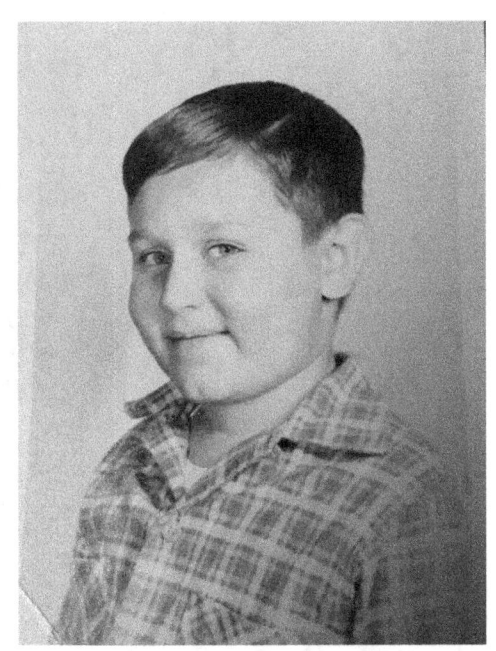

Above: Bobby Theiss, Age 2.
Right: Bobby Theiss, Age 8.
Courtesy of Jeffrey Mark Bruce

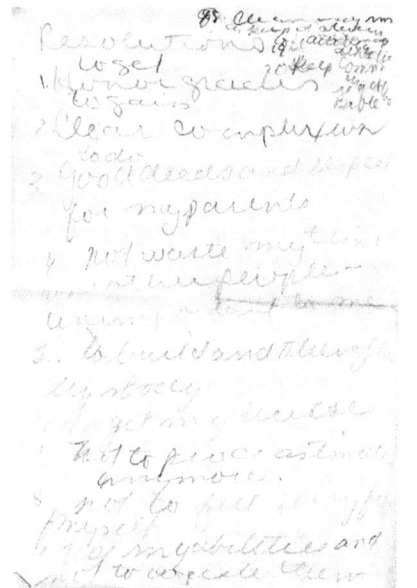

Bobby Theiss' 20 New Year's Resolutions for 1964.

Bob Theiss in the Air Force, 1969.
Courtesy of Jeffrey Mark Bruce

Bob Theiss stationed in Korea during the Vietnam War, circa 1969.
Courtesy of Jeffrey Mark Bruce

Robert Theiss in Korea.
Courtesy of Jeffrey Mark Bruce

Dugan's Bistro.
Courtesy of Gay Life Newspaper, Your Style Publications

The Bearded Lady.
Top two pictures: Gay Chicago, courtesy of the Legacy Project collection
Bottom two pictures: Courtesy of Darr Gapshis

BL and Peter Thompson.
Courtesy of Darr Gapshis

Lou DiVito (standing), Eddie Dugan and TL Noble.
Gay Chicago, courtesy of the Legacy Project collection

Eddie Dugan, BL, and turkeys.
Photo courtesy of Gerald Pagorek

dugan's 2nd New Year
at chicago's bar of the seventies
the bistro "the home of the bearded lady"
New Year's Eve December 31st 1974

Bistro business card. The Home of the Bearded Lady.

Eddie, Ron Veltman, and the upside-down Christmas tree.
Gay Chicago, courtesy of the Legacy Project collection

Lou DiVito with his gold record.
Gay Chicago, courtesy of the Legacy Project collection

The Bistro's 6th annivesary draped in 1,000 miles of mylar ribbon.
Courtesy of Daniel Goss

BL and several co-workers partying at Eddie Dugan's condo.
Courtesy of Daniel Goss

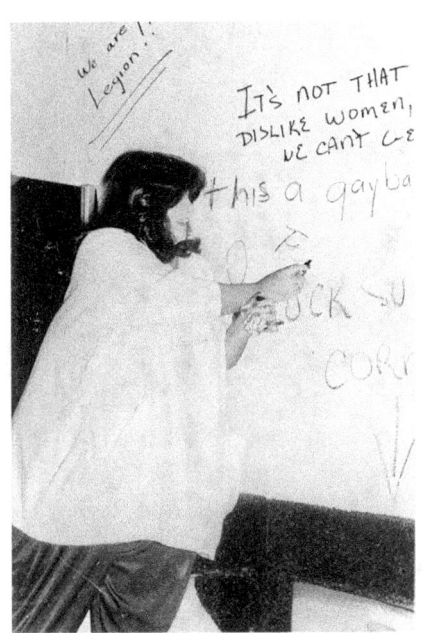

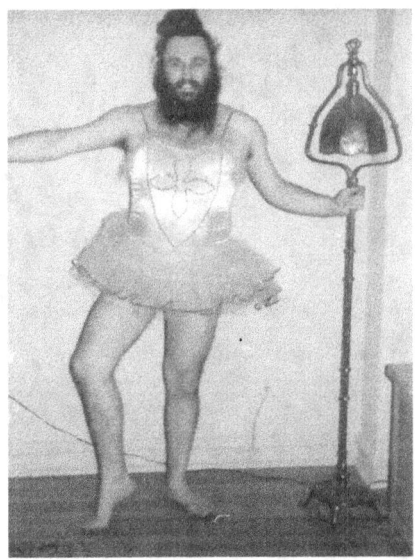

Photo of BL courtesy of Darr Gapshis

Janet Johnson.
Gay Chicago, courtesy of the Legacy Project collection

Bistro brick.
Courtesy of Daniel Goss

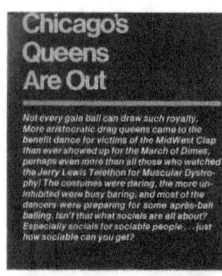

Left: From Club Quest The Multi-Sexual Review, July, 1977. Above: The Bearded Lady and Oh! Those Pants! t-shirt. Oct. 1, 1977.

From Vanidades Continental, March 17, 1975, the Venezuelan branch of Vanidades.

Farewell, Bistro.
Courtesy of GayLife Newspaper, YourStyle Publications.

Eddie in front of Paradise exterior.
Courtesy of Jimmy D'Ambrosia

Paradise renovation.
Courtesy of Darr Gapshis

Paradise poppers!
Courtesy of Jimmy D'Ambrosia

BL and Jeff.
Courtesy of Marc Hauser

BL and Jeff.
Courtesy of Jeffrey Mark Bruce

Advertisement for a production of A Funny Thing Happened on the Way to the Forum. The only time BL appeared on stage under his real name, Robert Theiss.

BL in the Theiss/Bruce home in Tokyo.
Photo courtesy of Jeffrey Mark Bruce

BL when he appeared on Oprah.

Left: Tuba and Clarinet Bunny. Right: BL performing in Tokyo.
Courtesy of Jeff Bruce

BL and Lon.
Courtesy of Lon Ellenberger

The postcard for BL's art show at the Earth Art Gallery in Tokyo, 1990.

BL at the Great Wall of China, 1985.

BL in Tokyo Orchid Garden.
Photo courtesy of Jeffrey Mark Bruce

The final photo taken of BL, his Alien Registration I.D. card.

> Memorial Service
> *oshoshiki*
>
> for Robert W. Theiss, Jr.
>
> 7:00 p.m., June 21, 2003
>
> at the home of Robert Theiss
> Yamato Heights 101
> 2-14-23 Takamatsu, Toshima-ku
> Tokyo, Japan
>
> -offering of prayers & condolences
>
> -reading of the eulogy and the history of the Theiss family
>
> -guest registry
>
> -photographs of the life & family of Robert Theiss
>
> -food and drinks served to guests following the service
>
> -the music of Lon Ellenberger
>
> -fans & Missoni handkerchiefs in memory of Robert Theiss
>
> -floral arrangements from friends and co-workers

Right: Card from Robert W. Theiss Jr.'s Memorial Service.

Below: Some of BL's remaining ashes were eventually inurned in the Columbarium Wall at Chicago's Graceland Cemetery.

Bronze head of the Bearded Lady by sculptor Claude Descoteaux (1983).
Photo courtesy of Jeffrey Mark Bruce

The author with a poster signed by BL.

I Will Survive

The friction between BL and his coworkers never fully abated after his return to the Bistro in 1975. Indeed, the truce proved to be temporary. In the late 1970s, things reached a tipping point again. While discussing the Bistro Christmas party in his *On Target* column for *Gay Chicago Magazine* [December, 1978], O.K. Boyz wrote, "Bearded Lady feeling the wrath! Not so smiley, these days. Only teeth. No sincerity. Maybe a new hair-do would perk up the once notorious lady. Or maybe a new act. Or something. Loved her party dress."

Things had escalated by spring of 1979. After not showing up to work one night, Eddie said he'd had enough. The "no show," combined with an increasingly bad attitude, caught up with BL. He was "dismissed" from the Bistro. As reported by Richard Cooke in the April 6th, 1979 issue of *GayLife*, "The Bearded Lady is no longer at the Bistro, but is involved with various bookings in Milwaukee and Detroit." Some felt Eddie had dismissed BL because he needed to learn he could be replaced.

BL hit the road and made the rounds over the next several months performing in Atlanta, Toronto, Cleveland, and Indianapolis (which he called Indianoplace). Among the places he performed was the multi-level and confetti-happy disco called "The Bar" in Champagne, IL. That evening, he soared high above the crowd on a swing and tossed goodies to patrons. As BL climbed the ladder to mount his lofty perch he was heard to murmur, "Even stars get scared sometimes." He may have been referring to more than a fear of falling.

Back in Chicago, BL did shows at The Ranch, sharing the stage with performers like Lisa Eaton, "more Judy Garland than Judy Garland;" Toni, who was touted as bringing back "a bit of the old Chesterfield;" and Lana, who was said to possess a "haunting beauty." He performed at Le Trolls and Darché, and also gave quite a performance at the Glory Hole. According the *GayLife*, "Alice in Wonderland would have been proud of the 'Fantasy

Panic at the Glory Hole,' what with the go-go boys, strangely familiarly-shaped balloons, the leather and fog rolling across the floor. The Bearded Lady appeared draped in plastic and left us all spellbound."

On Sundays and Mondays in the spring and summer of 1979, BL worked at the other major gay dance club in town, Carol's Speakeasy. The popular nightspot had re-opened after a major renovation mid-year and management was eager to lure back the gay nightlife crowd. One of the popular DJs at Carol's at the time was future Grammy Award winner Frankie Knuckles aka The Godfather of House Music. The bar took out full-page ads in the gay rags announcing the appearance of the Bearded Lady.

By late July, BL had told the Polish Princess, aka *GayLife* gossip columnist Ron Helizon, that he was "getting a whole new act together." BL liked seeing his name in the columns.

Around that same time in 1979 Steve Weil partnered with Eddie Dugan to bring some of that magical Bistro nightlife further north. On Friday, May 4th, 1979 the two men opened Coconuts at 5320 N. Sheridan, just north of Berwyn. The club's slogan was Eddie through and through: "Coconuts, for those who love the night life." The plaque in the entryway read, "Leave all your troubles at the door." For the new club, Steve would supply the capital. Eddie would bring the personality, the party atmosphere, and some of the talented Bistro people: bartenders, DJs, wait staff, and performers.

Wisely, throughout BL's reign at the Bistro, Eddie had cultivated an entire roster of uniquely talented performance artists; which meant that BL was not necessarily *the* star, but one of several non-traditional club superstars employed by the Bistro... acts that would now be performing at both the Bistro and Coconuts.

One of the most popular was a dancer/performance artist named "ILIB," which was his real name, Billy, misspelled backwards. Billy had a background in garment design and was a Bistro go-go boy before becoming a "personality." ILIB was tall, wore high heels, and usually dressed in silver. In his typical Kiss/Ziggy Stardust inspired make-up, ILIB's appearance was so jarring that he was once "taken in" for causing a public disturbance by simply walking down Michigan Avenue in full club regalia at 10:00AM.

Another popular Bistro/Coconuts personality was Greg "Kim" Spaulding, an innovative dancer who often performed in mime/clown regalia. Part drag queen and part Pierrot clown, Spaulding was fabulous, fond of designer clothes, and prone to striking poses beneath a strobe light. Kim had been a regular performer at the Bistro since 1977. He also had gigs working as a life-like mannequin in department store windows.

Bistro lighting guru and stage manager TL Noble also entertained regularly, dancing both in and out of drag. TL loved to make an entrance by turning his routines into production numbers – like his show stopping take on Sheila & B. Devotion's *Singing in the Rain.* TL performed the number beneath an umbrella after rigging a sprinkler to create a rain shower above the stage.

"Beluga" aka Michael Cegur started as a Bistro coat check boy, but was drawn to performing. Described as the "ménage a trois of sex, horror, and elegance," Beluga was fond of doing musical numbers that often segued into bloody massacres. According to Ralph Paul in a 1977 column in Gay Chicago News, Beluga created, "several still-discussed scandals including Murder By Plexiglass in which he ate dollar bills, flooded the discotheque, and inadvertently caused his partner to be hospitalized." A conceptual and avant-garde artist from Hammond, Indiana, Beluga is credited for introducing New Wave Theater to Chicago at La Mere Vipere.

Bistro crowds were also in awe of androgynous avant-garde performer "Vera Vinyl." Vera walked on broken glass and sometimes just stood on stage, striking an assortment of poses while maintaining an utterly blank facial expression. Shaved brows and heavy make-up made her look even more startling. Where BL was camp – Vera was deathly serious.

Danny "Dee Dee" Celebron filled the gap between camp and serious. Dee Dee was a trans dancer with a sometimes shaven head or short platinum hair and looked like a runway model. She loved wearing designer clothes and custom-made hats. Dee Dee threw fabulous poses to the music with her lanky shape.

Another Bistro/Coconuts talent was *Blueboy* magazine's Man of the Year 1981, Joseph LoPresti. Joe – who later changed his name to Hinmahtooyah – won numerous admirers dancing in his leather shorts and harness.

"Deluxe" was yet another popular member of the Bistro's roster of nightlife characters. Deluxe was an ambitious emcee and performer who wore wild muumuus and caftans. He was sometimes described as "Chicago's answer to Divine." Deluxe had a larger than life personality and a willingness to do anything. Although Deluxe was a solid emcee with a wonderful stage presence, he also possessed a devious streak. Sometimes he turned on people. Deluxe liked to stir the shit.

Despite long-standing friction with the entire Bistro Family – BL was also eventually invited to make the move to Coconuts. As reported in Richard Cooke's *DISCOvery* column in *GayLife*, "The Bearded Lady is now playing at Coconuts on Tuesday, Wednesday, Friday, and Saturday from 11:00PM til 2:00AM." Though BL frequently complained about things, by then the darkest period of his feud with Eddie had ended. Eddie knew that having BL move to Coconuts, instead of immediately returning to the Bistro, was a good way to boost business at his new club. It was also a way to keep Lou DiVito and BL separated; the two had been increasingly at odds prior to BL's dismissal.

Although he seemed as popular as ever at Coconuts, BL worried that someday Deluxe would replace him permanently. Given Deluxe's devious streak and BL's on-again off-again relationship with Eddie, BL's paranoia doesn't seem entirely ungrounded. Maybe BL's concern was based on something Deluxe said or did or perhaps it was the product of his own insecurity. Being the Bistro's top act for years, and collecting a *very* nice salary, meant something to BL. But fame came with concerns. Fans were fickle and a large part of being a "celebrity" was beyond his control.

Despite promises made to "the Polish Princess" (aka Ron

Helizon) that he was "getting a whole new act together," BL's routine at Coconuts was fairly uninspired. Mostly, he appeared looking outrageous, and danced a bit. But he did not typically perform on the main stage, which was reserved for special performances by musical acts and comics such as Evelyn "Champagne" King, Viola Wills, Sylvester, Michael Greer, and Pudgy.

Instead, BL performed on one of the smaller elevated "dance stages." Four small "performance platforms" were at each corner of the dance floor and lit by spotlights. When it was time to go on, BL simply stepped onto one of the two-and-a-half foot-high platforms and started dancing. At Coconuts BL continued his tradition of outrageous looks, like his headdress candelabra that flashed to the bass. Aside from his "look," BL mostly swayed to the beat.

Much of the magic BL had brought to his performances at the Bistro had vanished. He complained a lot. The gig bored him. The communal dressing room, which some evenings housed up to eight dancers, offered little to no privacy. The room was basically four chairs and a line of mirrors. Performers kept their costumes in the corner. Though his fans still inspired him, BL considered doing his set a chore. He missed the Bistro.

Coconuts was more brightly lit than the Bistro and offered dining as well as dancing. The club had a full menu: *Salad and Sandwiches from $3.95, Full Prime Rib Dinner $7.95*. Dining was offered from 6:00PM-10:00PM with some casual dancing on the floor. At 10:00PM, the food tables were whisked away, the lights lowered, the music grew louder, and the show started. The dance floor was a six-inch step up from a dining area that featured booths as well as tables. The DJ booth was a glass closet aside the relatively small dance floor. Reflective walls had a palm tree motif. Mannequins, painted as jungle animals, were placed throughout the bar. With a décor dominated by chrome and glass, Coconuts was meant to evoke the feel of a glamorous South American nightclub in an old movie.

But the club was plagued by problems. The primary issue

was its location. Many of the River North/Bistro crowd rarely ventured north of Belmont. Coconuts was twenty blocks north of that; another world entirely. The club also had problems with the law. Police occasionally harassed patrons entering and leaving the club. At Coconuts there was more fighting and friction among the clientele than ever occurred at the Bistro. It was a different vibe.

In September 1979, Ira Jones reported in *GayLife* that Eddie Dugan was doing terrific business at Coconuts. "It seems to be the 'in' place these days. Managed by our old friend Michael Anderson, Coconuts is the only successful straight/gay mixed facility in the Chicago area." The observation is a notable one. The predominantly gay vibe that Eddie always wanted at the Bistro was not in effect at Coconuts, though the outrageous element was often on display.

One community member recalls dining there with his boyfriend when BL approached the table and began flirting with the two young men. After some small talk, BL asked the two men for their underwear. Pulling a black Sharpie from the depths of his beard, he also requested that they sign them. The men dutifully went to the bathroom and removed their shorts. BL had their signed underwear in his hands by the time their salads were served.

Hopes for the new nightspot had been so high that briefly there was a satellite Coconuts, the ill-fated Coconut Grove, in Downers Grove. But, in spite a variety of approaches (Bratwurst Buffet, Date Night Dinner, Roast Pig Buffet, Oyster Bar, etc.) the restaurant portion of Coconuts never caught on. A full meal and a night of dancing were not a great mix. Management tried serving food after the dancing ended with a "4 until ??? Boogie Woogie Breakfast for $3.95 with a dessert bar and a juice bar." Promoted as "a way to become less severe," the breakfast idea proved to be a disappointment as well.

Despite some very fun holiday parties for Easter, Mardi Gras, Valentine's Day, Independence Day, and Halloween ("Whorer and Fear"); despite attracting celebrities like the Rolling Stones, Judy Tenuta, Seka, Jacqueline Bisset, Nell Carter, Walter Payton,

Margaux Hemingway, Paul Lynde, and Rock Hudson; and despite the work of top DJs like Frank Lipomi and Jeff Berry... Coconuts failed to duplicate the Bistro magic. The club ended up attracting more of a straight neighborhood crowd.

Coconuts opened in time to wish the Bistro a happy six-year anniversary. Bistro anniversary parties were always a happening, but the sixth anniversary was exceptional. In addition to a complete renovation, six mobile spotlights were set up outside of the bar, three on Dearborn and three on Hubbard, one for each year the Bistro had been in business.

For the sixth anniversary party, patrons were asked to dress in either black or white or both. The staff wore red. Before opening the doors, Eddie gathered the employees outside for the group picture. After a few photos, there was a bang. Mylar ribbon shot from the roof, streaming across Dearborn and Hubbard. Cars swerved to avoid the tangle as over 1,000 miles of ribbon were launched to celebrate. The festivities also included 100 pounds of glitter. Patrons noticed a few flakes of glitter a block away, then a dusting, then a layer covered the sidewalk. By the time they reached the Bistro door the red glitter was ankle deep.

New York impressionist Allan Lozito (who performed at the Bistro as Sister Very Too Much, Consuela Lopez, and Spermola) was quoted by the *Chicago Tribune* as saying, "Who else [but Dugan] could put a thousand miles of mylar ribbon down the outside of a building and cover a corner with glitter – right across the street from a police station?"

The sixth anniversary bash reportedly included enough white frosted cake to serve 1,000 people. The Bistro had transcended the description of mere disco. By the sixth anniversary, the Bistro became a self-proclaimed UltraDisco ("Traveling at...The Speed of Sound.")

The relationship between BL and the Bistro folks was still strained at the time of the sixth anniversary extravaganza, but BL seemed to have learned his lesson. He missed working there and he missed his fans. BL showed up for the Bistro party, but he arrived wearing pants. By December of 1979 BL was back at the Bistro and better than ever. In *GayLife*, Richard Cooke reported on BL's exceptional performance saying, "It had to be seen to be believed and it was the highlight of the evening."

That December, BL also appeared at the legendary New York disco G.G. Barnum's Room, where handsome male dancers performed on a trapeze above the dance floor. Though BL was a hit with the crowd, the engagement was limited. BL had a wild time in New York. He especially enjoyed the hardcore leather/sex bars, like the parade of flesh at the Anvil and the extreme decadence of the Mineshaft. BL's motto was the sleazier the better. Some nights BL partied a little too hard. One night, after a G.G. Barnum's performance, a trip to the leather bars, and some hallucinogens, BL put his six-inch stiletto heel through the plastic divider shield of a taxicab. He was forced to pay for the damages and was promptly dropped at the curb.

BL returned to Chicago with a triumphant "coming home" party at the Bistro. Shortly after his return, Eddie gave in to one of his demands and supplied a limo to chauffeur BL to and from the club. The rocky patch between the two men seemed over. BL was home just in time to ring in the new decade. The 1980s had arrived.

Last Dance

Though the cash was flowing and disco was enormously popular, not everyone was a fan. Chicago DJ Steve Dahl had been fired from WDAI-FM when the station switched to an all-disco format. WDAI was also the station that featured Lou DiVito as a DJ. Dahl had a score to settle and he vowed to end what he called "Disco Dystrophy," referring to WDAI as "Disco - D.I.E." When disco star Van McCoy died suddenly of a heart attack on July 6, 1979, Dahl honored the occasion by destroying McCoy's recording of *The Hustle* on the air.

Dahl's "cause" reached its peak on July 12, 1979, when he championed Disco Demolition Night at Comiskey Park. That evening folks were admitted to the White Sox and Detroit Tigers double-header for 98 cents if they brought a disco record. Between games, amidst cries of "Death to Disco," Dahl blew up a crate of disco records. The act prompted thousands of rioters to storm the field, vandalizing the park and hurling vinyl discs like Frisbees. In the end over three-dozen were arrested, the Sox playing field was destroyed, and the game was forfeited.

Hatred for a genre of music, with clear hints of homophobia and racism, had been ignited in the public. Hating disco became a cause. The 1980s were destined to be a very different decade, not only for music, but also for the LGBT community. A greater and more formidable monster than Steve Dahl would strike the community in the coming months.

The Bistro was a snapshot in time, a happening, a party. But – in spite of Eddie Dugan's herculean efforts – parties don't last forever. The writing was on the wall. In the months prior to its eventual closing, property values in the River North area were on the rise and the neighborhood began to get "cleaned up." The Bistro still had lines down the block on weekends when the building at 420 N. Dearborn was sold to a Canadian firm, just one year before Eddie had the option of renewing his 10-year lease. The party was over.

The Bistro had fallen victim to the North Loop Development Project. Prior to the end, Eddie and the staff had sometimes worn t-shirts that said, "There's No Place Like the Bistro." Once the closing of the club was inevitable, new t-shirts were printed that read, "There's No Place Like the Bistro Anymore." The world-famous club closed on May 31st, 1982... actually at 4:00AM on June 1st. The building was vacated. Demolition started on June 3rd.

In early May, Eddie spoke with *GayLife*. "All good things must eventually come to an end, but it is especially difficult for me to announce that the Bistro will close May 31, nine years to the day that the doors of the Midwest's first major disco opened." Discussing the demolition, Eddie added, "They will not be able to destroy the memories of myself, my staff, and the hundreds of thousands of persons who visited the Bistro during the past nine years. At times, 1973 seems like only a short time ago, but when I look back at the photos of some of the events held here at the Bistro, I realize that the nine-year life of the Bistro was fun-filled. The Bistro truly became a place to party, a place to dance, and a place to meet people. I'm proud of some of the innovative moves we made at the Bistro, and I'm especially proud of the lead we took in providing Chicago and the Midwest with the best in sound and lights. I'll miss the Bistro. It has been my baby for the past nine years, but we're going to move ahead." In closing, Eddie wished to thank his parents, his business partners, his staff, and most of all his patrons. "Without the customers, the Bistro would never have become a premiere disco."

Given the grim news, Eddie decided to do what he did best. On May 31st, the disco's 9th anniversary, Dugan threw a party with a Black and White theme. The final night at the Bistro was a party to end all parties with, according to the *Chicago Tribune*, over 2000 people in attendance. As with the eighth anniversary bash, there were six different cakes, each adorned with a letter that spelled out the word L-E-G-E-N-D. The party was actually the culmination of a seven-night farewell bash which had included surprise performances and appearances and a heightened level of debauchery that included openly doing cocaine off the back bar.

Four days later wrecking balls from the Cleveland Wrecking Company demolished "the Studio 54 of Chicago." The day was cold and drizzly. The Bistro walls fell in a cloud of dust, but within the haze was a shimmer. Gold, red, and silver glitter sparkled on the sidewalk and in the gutters that rainy day. Some said it was in the walls. Others suspect someone left a few bags of glitter in the building to add sparkle to the plume of destruction dust: a final Bistro hurrah.

Although Dugan's Bistro had been his stepping-stone to notoriety, BL wasn't terribly emotional about the closing. He was more pragmatic about his career. Rumors circulated that BL was at the demolition site, eager to be photographed on what remained of the Bistro's stage. Crews refused to let him cross the caution line. Instead, BL posed for some shots of the ruins from the sidewalk.

Supposedly the rush to tear down the building was due to an urgency to erect a luxury high rise, but the lot sat empty for years. In the end, the Bistro, ground zero of much of the Chicago LGBT community's outrageousness, became another parking lot.

Eddie was devastated to lose the bar. He confessed he could have run the Bistro for the rest of his life. The day after the demolition, Eddie, Lou, and TL sifted through the rubble for 100 unbroken bricks. Eddie wanted to distribute them as mementos. He wanted some of his favorite people to have a piece of that magical place. The bricks were numbered 1-100 with attached brass plates that said: *There's No Place Like The Bistro. Thanks, Love, Eddie*. He called the bricks, Bistro Headstones.

In the June 4, 1982, issue of *GayLife*, Bistro lawyer and Dugan cohort Ron Ehemann dedicated his entire Speaking Of column to the closing of the Bistro:

> "An era ends—after nine years as one of the flagships of the night, Dugan's Bistro succumbed to the wrecking ball and 'progress.'

"Whether you were a 'Bistro Bunny' or not, most everyone had been through the doors. Dignitaries and celebrities, young and old -- part of being in gay Chicago involved at least one night at the Bistro.

"While I can't say the Bistro was my first gay bar, it was certainly among them. Like so many other people, I will always retain some very special memories of nights spent there. Thus, though it doesn't fit my usual format, I think it appropriate to express my personal thoughts on the closing of the bar.

"Most eulogies tend to overlook faults. We canonize the deceased and praise rather than criticize. The Bistro had its share of complaints, its share of 'attitude' and its share of controversy. But the Bistro had something else; a mystique and atmosphere, not unlike New York's infamous Studio 54. Though some felt the door policy was too harsh, one thing that was always excluded was depression.

"Eddie Dugan understood how to throw a party. He understood how to take a crowd and work it until people forgot their troubles, threw care to the wind, and enjoyed themselves. Eddie also knew how to make you feel important, part of the "in crowd." That's what opened the doors nine years ago when others thought it was foolish to attempt anything on such a scale, and that's what kept the doors open while others came and went. Together with the Gold Coast, the Bistro became internationally known as a gay landmark in the Midwest.

"The Bistro was Eddie Dugan. It was

created as much by him as he by it; they were inseparably bound. The mood you might have found on any given night most probably reflected Eddie's personal mood as well.

"It's difficult to single out one person, particularly when the city is filled with so many. There are bars and bar owners with much more community involvement, much more personal contact. But there are few who achieved the sense of charisma surrounding Eddie Dugan or the Bistro.

"Contributing to the success of the Bistro were hundreds of employees over the years—dedicated people who worked while we partied. These were the people who suffered during the Bistro's recent liquor license suspension. Though each added a valuable part of themselves to the bar, much of the energy and creativity came from Tommy [TL] Noble, Lou DiVito and Ronny Veltman. The Bistro was also responsible for bringing us such entertainers as the Bearded Lady, Kim [Spaulding], and Deluxe.

"If there are lessons to be drawn from the Bistro they concern visibility and magnitude. The Bistro showed us that we can carry things off on a grand scale, that we can be visible and loud. The 'UltraDisco' was never quiet about its presence across from one of the largest police stations in Chicago. Red glitter and spotlights, neither the Bistro nor the gay community was ever hidden at Hubbard and Dearborn Streets.

"Door policy notwithstanding, the Bistro was one of those rare places where gay and non-gay merged. Eddie Dugan once told me,

'The Bistro isn't a gay bar, it's a party, and the guests don't have to be anything but fun.

"There is another lesson we can learn from the Bistro and its demise: Once you have it, you don't have to give it up.

"'Progress' and changing times may cause physical things to pass, but nothing stops us from moving onward and upward. Though the Bistro is gone, Paradise is rising from the ashes of the Phoenix."

Ron Ehemann, 1982

Never Knew Love Like This Before

On March 8, 1982, 28 year-old Jeff Bruce arrived in Chicago for a job interview. That night Jeff decided to go to the Bistro. When he arrived, the bar was in full swing. The Bistro had been temporarily closed following another liquor violation. The reopening party, with complimentary cocktails, drew a mammoth crowd.

That night BL was especially energized. He had taken advantage of the closing and went on a brief museum and shopping excursion to Amsterdam with best friend, Carol Cheeseman. When BL saw Jeff at the bar that night, he noticed Jeff wasn't drinking. Jeff said it was too crowded to get the bartender's attention. BL asked what he wanted and snapped a finger. Soon Jeff was being plied with strong cocktails.

Although the number of people who knew BL impressed him, Jeff wasn't aware of BL's celebrity when he met him. He had mentioned the initials, but Jeff didn't ask what they stood for. Although BL enjoyed being famous, he also liked that it wasn't something Jeff knew or cared about.

Jeff went home with BL that first night. Though the March temperatures that evening dipped into the single digits, that didn't stop them from enjoying a brief bit of naked fun outside BL's Uptown apartment building. BL may have also been gauging Jeff to see how great a risk taker he was. Evidently Jeff passed the test.

Within two months, BL was visiting Jeff at his place in Flint, Michigan where Jeff taught at a community college. Wanting to show Jeff he was a hard worker, BL got out a rotary mower and cut the grass while Jeff was teaching. After he finished mowing, BL walked over and had a beer with Jeff's factory worker neighbors. When Jeff asked BL what the neighbors thought of him, BL said, "They thought I was just third shift, on drugs."

BL wanted this relationship to work. The Bistro was closing and things weren't working out at Coconuts. He needed a change. He'd been a club celebrity for nine years. Jeff was moving to

Japan very soon and BL wanted to move there with him. He'd been eager to return to Asia since being stationed in Korea.

Trouble in Paradise

At the time of the Bistro's closing, Eddie was already in the process of opening an even bigger club, the 25,000 square foot mega-disco Paradise aka Paradise Island at 2848 N. Broadway. The club was a joint venture with Eddie and business partner Steve Weil. Since 1976 the North Broadway space had been the Phoenix. As Ron Ehemann said in his *GayLife* column, Paradise was indeed rising from the ashes of the Phoenix.

No expense was spared in the design of Paradise, which required a complete gutting of the previous interior. Paradise opened in three "phases." By summer 1982, the front bar [Phase 1] had opened. Phase 2 was completed by September. By October, $50 Paradise memberships were being sold. Completion of the project, with the Paradise Ballroom [Phase 3] and a full opening, was slated for November 1982.

Eddie vowed Paradise would have the best sound, the best technology, an enormous stage, and a "Rolls Royce of a DJ booth." The high ceiling at Paradise allowed Eddie to mimic a favorite Studio 54 feature, a state-of-the-art moveable lighting effect, operated by hydraulics. The collection of lights, devices, and gadgets moved up and down on an enormous pentagon-shaped truss. One Sunday night in June of 1984, the winch, which carried the cables up and down, failed. The truss dropped several feet, hitting one woman on the shoulder. Miraculously, she was not seriously injured.

Paradise had a front bar adjoined to a dining area, the Paradise Alley Café, with "three-dimensional replicas of a fire station, tenement style back porches, and an elevated train platform" [Ron Grossman, the *Chicago Tribune*]. The menu was fairly basic: pizza, sandwiches, fries, burgers, etc. At one of the corner tables, Divine once ate plate after plate of ribs before taking two more orders to go.

Beyond the restaurant was a hallway dubbed "The Alley," an urban themed passage decorated with a subway mural, graffiti, and a chain link fence. Hanging high above that portion of the club was the old Dugan's Bistro sign. Adjacent to the alley was the coat check, a smaller dance floor, and a DJ booth. This dance area had a sky roof and was the site of the Sunday afternoon tea dances, one of the most popular features of Paradise.

The Alley led to the enormous ballroom with three more bars. Above the dance floor and shaped like a spaceship, was the main DJ booth which was accessed by a spiral staircase. Stairs off the dance floor led to the game room on the second floor with pool tables and video games.

A curving grand staircase led to the VIP lounge that was encased in glass and overlooked the dance floor. The lounge was plush with a padded bar, sofas, seashell chairs, and cocktail tables. Birds of Paradise, the "official flower of the club," were showcased about the bar.

Thelma Houston performed at Paradise for opening night, December 21, 1982. Gold and Sneed's *INC.* column in the *Chicago Tribune* reported, "Other acts lined up opening week include Sylvester, Sharon Redd, Spyyse, and Claudja Barry."

Viola Wills played there on New Year's Eve. The Weather Girls, Paul Parker, Lime (*Babe, We're Gonna Love Tonight*), Debbie Jacobs (*Don't You Want My Love*), Boys Town Gang (*Ain't No Mountain High Enough*), Jayne Edwards (*It Should Have Been Me*), Cynthia Manley, Pamala Staney, Linda Clifford, Jimmy Sommerville, Carol Douglas (*Doctor's Orders*) and Eartha Kitt (promoting her dance single *Where Is My Man?*), were among the entertainers who graced the Paradise stage.

The disco showplace had a nightly staff of anywhere from 50-70. Most advertisements for the club included the catchphrase, "There's No Such Thing as a Stranger in Paradise." The busiest nights at Paradise tended to be Thursdays ($1 drinks), Sundays (tea dance), and, as expected, Friday and Saturdays. The rest of the nights were spotty. The enormous space required more than a decent-sized crowd to not appear empty.

In 1984, Eddie had his 38th birthday party at Paradise. Like his previous birthday bashes, it was spectacular. The theme was *The Wizard of Oz*. When he arrived, Eddie was given a pair of ruby slippers and told to follow the yellow brick road, which led to the dance floor. The club had been reimagined as scenes from the movie. The first bar represented Kansas and was all in black and white. The coat check was the haunted forest with apples suspended from the ceiling. The VIP Lounge was decorated as Oz. The Witch's castle, with an enormous hourglass, was recreated in another area. Staffers were dressed as the Scarecrow, the Tin Man, the Cowardly Lion, Glinda, and of course the Wicked Witch of the West. Flying monkeys were recreated as well. As an added treat, lesbian disco legend Alicia Bridges was flown in to perform Eddie's anthem, *I Love the Nightlife*.

Like Dugan's previous clubs, Paradise attracted celebrities; Liza Minnelli, Elton John, Mayor Jane Byrne, Karen Black, Barry Gibb, Tina Turner, Andy Bell, Judy Tenuta, Andy Warhol, Grace Jones, Luther Vandross, Seka, Robert Conrad, Barbi Benton, Lynda Carter, Rip Taylor, Al Parker, Jacqueline Bisset, Carrie Fisher, Diana Ross, Andy Bell, Marilyn Sokol, Barry Manilow, and Johnny Mathis. One evening Wayland Flowers came in with his puppet Madame on his arm. Madame dropped her feather boa at coat check, and the two headed to the VIP lounge.

Despite the effort and considerable planning and expense, Paradise, like Coconuts, failed to capture the Bistro's magic. Some of it may have been the club or the location. However, timing may have been the biggest factor in the ultimate failure of Paradise…

On June 5, 1981 the CDC reported five cases of the rare lung infection PCP (Pneumocystis Carinii Pneumonia) in previously healthy gay men in Los Angeles. Though it didn't yet have a name, the AIDS crisis had begun. Whisperings of the "gay cancer" began appearing on either coast, growing louder each with passing month, and then every week. By spring of 1982 the "gay plague" was named GRID, Gay Related Immune Deficiency. In September 1982, before Paradise was even fully open, the term AIDS was used for the first time to describe the epidemic. A mere fifteen months had passed since the first reports of the disease had surfaced; only three months since the demise of the Bistro. The world – especially the club scene – was a very different place.

Some members of the gay community sensed the dark storm gathering and started to think about settling down. Others turned to drugs and alcohol to cope with their rising anxiety. By the mid-1980s, the atmosphere of dread was impossible to ignore. Paradise had become a different sort of wild. Though the party continued, the celebration had ended. Times were no longer carefree. The scene had become tinged with desperation and escape.

When the pipes backed up at Paradise, plumbers ran a hose to the street to drain them. After the pipes were cleared there was a mound of sludge in the street along with dozens of snow seal bags – waterproof pouches of coated paper used to carry cocaine – that had been the cause of the clogged pipes. What had been concealed behind the glitz and glamour of the Bistro was revealed for all to see at Paradise.

On New Year's Eve of 1985, Paradise was raided. The entertainer for the evening, Pamala Stanley, had not yet taken to the stage when the police arrived. Officers went directly to where Eddie kept his stash, above a ceiling tile in the office. However, someone must have tipped him off about the raid because nothing was there. Several patrons and employees had drugs in their possession and were arrested. During the "raid," officers broke things and dumped ashtrays into the ice. Some suspect the police were sending a message that they wanted more pay-off money.

Eddie was also taken to the Town Hall Station on drug charges. But before being taken away, he said, "Get my full length mink, the one with the pale blue lining. I'm going to make an entrance." Eddie spent the night in jail, but was not charged. It was the third raid for Paradise.

One patron, recalling the second raid, said; "I was sitting in the VIP lounge. All of a sudden I saw the bartenders and wait staff emptying their pockets and throwing their drugs into the garbage. They must have heard the cops were outside. Minutes later the cops came through the crowd, making their way upstairs. Whoever took out the garbage that night sure got a good tip."

Three drug raids was a significant number. Some claimed the neighborhood simply did not want that sort of nightclub. There were actual neighbors *living* in the Lakeview area east of Broadway. That had never been an issue in River North. Following the third raid, business partner, Steve Weil, took over the club.

Most attributed Eddie Dugan's departure to his escalating drug use. Before he walked away from Paradise, he wanted to throw one last party to announce that he was no longer a partner in the business. Each invitation to Eddie's "No Snow" party had a red circle with a slash through the center over the image of a snowman. The invite came with an empty snow seal bag.

The night of the party, Eddie filled the Nerf cannon with hundreds of snow seal bags. Before the cannon was fired Eddie hinted that one of the bags might be filled with cocaine. At the firing, the crowd scrambled onto the dance floor, ripping open snow seal after snow seal to find the packet with the coke inside. Lou DiVito found the prize packet.

With Eddie no longer involved in the running of Paradise, the personality, the spontaneity, and vitality of the club was gone. Without Eddie, the party was soon over. Paradise closed in spring of 1986. Ironically, the club space would again be reborn as a nightclub called the Phoenix.

Pleasure Island

Though they knew he was smitten with Jeff, some of BL's friends were taken by surprise when the couple moved to Tokyo in September of 1982. The relocation did not go smoothly. BL was not prone to preparation. Everything was last minute. He had far too much to move and wanted to take as much as possible. Though he could buy cosmetics in Japan, BL was adamant about bringing what he would need for performances, including his top-quality rubber tits and some layering outfits. To further weed his possessions, he decided all his future headdresses would be made with local flowers and materials.

Drug use was something else BL left behind when he moved to Japan. He was entering a different phase of his life, making a new start. Japan had very strict drug laws at the time. An arrest would mean immediate deportation. The buzz wasn't worth the risk.

After their arrival in Tokyo, Jeff and BL attended a Halloween costume competition. BL won the contest and the attention of a nightclub owner who invited him to entertain at a private birthday party for Stevie Wonder. At the event, BL went to the mirrored men's room to touch up his make-up, but didn't realize his primping mirror was also a stall door. Stevie was at a urinal across the room. When the stall door opened, Wonder's bodyguard emerged, and shouted that a woman was in the men's room. Stevie panicked, turned, and pissed on the floor. The bodyguard turned Stevie back towards the urinal, and said it was his mistake. He told the superstar he'd explain later.

In Tokyo, BL attempted to pursue the sort of performance work he'd done in Chicago, but the environment was different. Virtually every gay club in Tokyo at the time was tiny, with room for no more than 30 or 40 patrons and a small six-stool bar with one bartender. Tokyo's gay district – No-chome – had dozens of tiny gay bars lining a four-block radius. There BL would appear on the street and cause a scene. People would come out of the bars just to see this curious man. Given his size, that was just as well. BL dominated many spaces. Some bars were too small for him. Other bars denied him admission because of the language barrier. This had less to do with xenophobia than with the bar master (as bar owners are called in Japan) not being able to communicate with him as a patron.

Japan had a rich heritage of drag embedded in the culture, both in theater and the arts. However, traditional geisha drag was nothing like Western drag and certainly nothing like BL's particular form of Western drag. His accessories alone were a sensation. BL wore rings on every finger, sometimes more than one, as well as numerous necklaces, broaches, and fancy belts with bold buckles.

BL adored looking "put together." He considered dressing up to be his patriotic duty as an American. By taking pains with his appearance he was countering the notion that all Americans ran around in torn jeans and jogging suits. BL vowed his wardrobe would never include ragged jeans or a jogging suit.

Eventually, BL signed with a booking agent and performed at various events in town. Being booked at a bar or club was rare. Most of BL's Tokyo gigs were private parties with an occasional larger format show. For a change of pace, BL even appeared in a stage production of *A Funny Thing Happened on the Way to the Forum*, performing under his real name, Bob Theiss. In the play, BL played the brothel owner.

In his party and event appearances, BL typically did one or two numbers throughout the evening. Mostly he did what he knew. BL came out wearing a kimono and beneath it was a layering of three, perhaps four more kimonos. His music had changed. No more *Love's Theme* and *Who's That Lady*. Now BL would primarily lip-synch to popular songs. Cher was his favorite. At most places he performed in Tokyo, there wasn't adequate room for him to dance. At larger venues, he brought a Japanese muscleman or two to gyrate behind him.

His hair creations were still excessive, often adding a foot or more to his height. The impact was even greater given BL's love of platform shoes. His hairpieces prompted gasps and oftentimes an eruption of applause. Most of these gorgeous, colorful creations featured ikebana, or traditional Japanese flower arranging. During his performance not a flower or prop shifted. Sometimes his floral arrangements and hair props incorporated wires and metal that hurt his scalp to the point of bleeding. BL reasoned that almost any amount of discomfort was worth it if the result was fabulous.

The sporadic nature of performance work in Tokyo frustrated him. He might perform once a week, then have no gigs for a month, followed by three bookings the next month. The inconsistency made budgeting problematic and given BL's love of shopping, a steady stream of income was essential.

Since full-time performance work was not an option, BL sought other avenues of employment. He began teaching English as a Second Language and discovered he was good at it. As an instructor he was both popular and effective in the classroom. He liked to pantomime and emote. BL had more action and drama in his lessons than 99% of ESL instructors. He was pleased to discover that teaching was simply another sort of performance, one with a salary and a captive audience.

BL adored Tokyo. The city suited his fondness for exploring and his inability to drive. The metropolis had a wonderful public transportation system and BL enjoyed walking. He didn't even learn how to ride a bicycle until he was fifty.

In Tokyo, BL derived enormous pleasure discovering new neighborhoods, going down each street, and inside every shop. Nothing pleased him more than meeting a friend for coffee before heading out for an afternoon of shopping. At Japanese department stores, BL liked to admire the high-end kimonos and obi (kimono sashes) as well as various accessories. He also enjoyed thrift shopping, looking for items in smaller shops, and bargaining with owners for whatever caught his fancy.

Pawnshops were another passion. In Japanese culture there was a tradition of businessmen and patrons going into various high-end dining and drinking establishments and having a host or hostess serve them. The patron would visit these people regularly, bringing the host/hostess an offering of gifts, sometimes quite expensive ones - jewelry, handbags, kimonos, wallets, etc. Since living conditions in Tokyo were cramped, the host/hostesses often took these gifts to certain pawnshops for money. BL became familiar with the shops that specialized in such things and found some wonderful bargains there.

Tokyo museums thrilled BL. He enjoyed weekly excursions to museums and gallery exhibitions. Teien Art Museum in the Meguro section of Tokyo was his favorite. The museum itself was an art deco house built by Emperor Hirohito's younger brother who had studied architecture in Paris and decided that his place in Japanese society would be to build the finest art deco home in the country.

BL also enjoyed the Nezu Museum, an art museum formerly known as the Nezu Institute of Fine Arts. He especially enjoyed museums with an Asian art focus. When something interested BL, he was voracious to learn all that he could about it. He eventually returned to school, majoring in the History of Art and Architecture with an emphasis on Asian Art.

Given his broad range of interests, it isn't surprising that BL also appreciated Tokyo's various offbeat museums, such as Meguro Parasitological Museum, a medical museum where the 300 specimens on display included the world's longest tapeworm.

The antiquity and traditions of Japanese culture fascinated BL. He enjoyed the vibrancy of life in Tokyo and the openness of its people. BL loved being approached on the street. Older Japanese women frequently stopped him to admire his jewelry or shoes. BL knew the story behind every item he wore and made sure every piece he owned was unique and well crafted. He took pleasure in being a walking and breathing piece of art. Being approached and admired amused him to no end and pressed him to try even harder to make an impression. He considered the act of doing so a way of making the world a nicer and more interesting place.

The Second Time Around

In 1985 – after three years of sporadic performing, studying Japanese, teaching English, and shopping – a call came from Chicago with a job offer. A revamped version of Coconuts was opening. *Would he be interested in performing there?* After some discussion, Jeff and BL decided to return to Chicago. That summer, BL went to work at the resurrected Coconuts and in the fall Jeff went to Northwestern for his Masters degree.

The original Coconuts had closed in 1983. In the 18 months that followed the closing, the concept and business plan was revised. The new Coconuts moved from North Sheridan to 5246 N. Broadway. Now it was more of a straight-out dance club. The nightspot was not aiming to lure high-end clientele anymore. They were looking for the party crowd; the people who would spend money seven days a week. They wanted BL back.

Dugan spoke to the *Chicago Tribune* in 1985 about the feel of the new Coconuts, comparing it to the city's current jet-setter nightspot, the Limelight, which had just opened. "Chicago simply doesn't have enough celebrities or 'party people' to make this city's Limelight anything like the New York club." Dugan said the most successful Chicago clubs are neighborhood bars that depend on the regulars to carry the business during the week. "People don't party in Chicago during the week like they do in New York. They don't spend their money as freely here and they pick their nights to go out. You have to think about your weekday business. Are people going to go to the Limelight on a Tuesday night with 20 inches of snow on the ground, or are they going to go to their neighborhood bar?"

In addition to Coconuts, BL also worked briefly as one of the "living art pieces" at the Limelight in Chicago. The grand opening of the club, on July 31, 1985, drew such celebrities as Andy Warhol and Tony Bennett. That night BL arrived at the 40,000 square foot, three-story, 3.5 million dollar club at Dearborn and Ontario in a carriage drawn by two white horses. In the *Chicago Tribune*,

Warhol was quoted as calling the Limelight opening, "The party of the year."

The Limelight was hyped as, "a return to art, and a return to glamour." As one of the art pieces, BL was relegated to one of the glass performance cases along the main corridor where his primary task was to "give attitude" and add to the club's "carnivalesque" appeal. BL could give attitude; the challenge was keeping him in his case. He wanted to come out and talk to people, dance, and go to the bar. At the Limelight, he preferred spending his time on a dais in the Dome Room surrounded by friends and admirers. In 1986, the Limelight named him "Queen of the Nightclubs" in a citywide contest. The Limelight eventually closed on New Years Eve, 1989, with a final night's performance by Cab Calloway. The space eventually became the club, Excalibur. During this period, BL also worked occasionally at Club Victoria and Paradise, but his primary gig was Coconuts.

BL's second Coconuts experience was different than it had been before. The three preceding years had brought enormous changes. At 38, BL was more settled. He was also drug-free and less frantic in his day-to-day life. Disco was dead. The crowd was different as well. With Eddie at the helm, Coconuts had a strong LGBT appeal, but it was not specifically gay. Even if it had been, the community had been radically altered in the last few months. In the 1970s, police harassment had fostered camaraderie in the newly liberated community. That wasn't the main issue anymore.

By the mid-1980s AIDS had begun to decimate Chicago's gay population and its specter cast a pall upon the community. Countless numbers of Bistro customers, bartenders, and staff died during the pandemic. Eddie Dugan, the life of the party, died of AIDS at age 40 on April 10, 1987 in the midst of the construction of Bistro Too, a new club he was opening with Chuck Renslow and Ron Ehemann. Bistro Too opened two months later in June.

As per Eddie's wishes, *I Love the Nightlife* played repeatedly at his visitation as dozens of relatives and friends passed by the open casket and dropped flower petals inside. At the service a statement by Eddie was read asking his friends to think of him at those times when they were having the most fun, at parties.

At the time, Dugan's mother, Helen Davison, had this to say about her son. "Eddie was unique and one-of-a-kind person. In his short life he brought joy, pleasure, and help to more people than most would have done in 80 years. He loved the nightlife and he loved his many friends. His father, Ed and I, appreciate them all, especially those who stayed close to him and us near the end." Contributions were made in Eddie's name to the AIDS hospice of Illinois Masonic Hospital. He is buried in Memory Gardens Cemetery in Arlington Heights. On his grave marker are his name, birth and death dates, and a lion to honor his Leo zodiac sign.

When Lou DiVito started getting sick he became reclusive, only allowing a few close friends to visit him. On September 18, 1991, AIDS claimed the life of the DJ extraordinaire, the man who brought the music and the crowds to the Bistro dance floor. Lou was 39.

At Coconuts, BL worked Tuesdays and Wednesdays, Fridays and Saturdays from 11:00PM – 2:00AM. Despite the profound social changes, he resumed his act as though nothing had happened. Rather than being yesterday's news, he was almost as popular as ever. Many yearned for nostalgia and escape. With the onslaught of AIDS, life had changed so dramatically that even something from three years earlier already felt like part of a different era. The one thing that had changed was that BL began to emcee more. He was not especially skilled at ad-libbing, but he possessed a unique charm and was wonderful at getting the crowd's attention. His primary duty was introducing acts to the stage.

In Sukie de la Croix's Chicago Whispers column in *Windy City Times*, dancer James recalled working with BL at Coconuts, "The Bearded Lady was our evil den mother, pretty wild. He was a different person out of drag, I'll tell you that. He was extremely low key, just like a motorcycle-looking kind of guy. His persona came when he was starting to get dressed, putting on his five pairs of stockings. He was really protective of me and he would scream at people who got within 10 feet of me, 'Stay away from my straight husband,' and he would stomp his feet. It was just a big act and he was hysterical."

Many nights Jeff would walk BL to work. He often needed assistance toting the bags with his props and outfits for the evening. Sometimes Jeff helped him get ready, but he rarely stayed for the show. Jeff taught at National College in the Loop most mornings. The couple frequently had breakfast together before Jeff went to work, and BL headed for bed.

Once BL stepped in the door at Coconuts, he was all business. Many of his fellow performers were wrapped up in backstage melodrama. BL understood. He had seen – and had certainly contributed to – a great deal of it in his earlier years; but in the interim he had learned when to turn it off and when to turn it on. "Save the drama for the stage," he liked to say to the younger dancers and entertainers.

At Coconuts, BL got to know many of the regulars. Living abroad had made him extremely comfortable with a wide cultural mix. His ease at overlooking ethnic barriers combined with his outgoing personality to make him well suited for the gig. He was especially fond of the many Arab customers. However, when Arab patrons got fresh, BL had no problem putting them in their place by retorting, "This isn't downtown Bagdad!"

In February 1986, BL appeared on *The Oprah Winfrey Show* in an episode about New York based "celebutantes," as club personalities were called at the time. By that point BL had been a celebutante for over a dozen years. He wasn't on the panel, but had a prominent seat in the audience. On the show, he stood, wearing "daytime BL regalia," and asked the panel: "What do you do when you're out of the spotlight? What do you do at home?" Given the changes in his life and the world he had known, BL's question seemed especially reflective. Oprah looked overwhelmed by it all.

In autumn 1986, BL enrolled at the University of Illinois-Chicago with studies in Art and Architecture. He was confident about wanting to return to college to complete his degree. He took several classes on Asian Art and consistently knew more on the subject than anyone in the class – sometimes even more than the professor. Two years later, BL received his bachelor's degree in Art History.

Once Bistro Too opened, BL started going there. He shared with friends that frequenting a place that was supposed to have been part Eddie's and that carried the Bistro name was haunting, but seeing some familiar Bistro faces was nice. The Bistro mainstays on staff included TL Noble, who did some of the artwork and design at the new club as well as performed (most notably Natalie Cole's *Pink Cadillac* on the hood of a car that came through a backdrop on stage!), dancer Kim Spaulding, DJ Jeff Berry, and club co-owner Ron Ehemann.

On June 12, 1988, the same day BL graduated from the university, one of his closest friends from the Bistro and Coconuts, bartender Peter Thompson, died of a heart attack at Columbus Hospital after a long illness. For months beforehand, BL and Jeff visited the bedridden Peter and brought videos to watch. At the end of his life Peter was unable to speak, and had only a feeding tube. After his passing, Jeff and BL were in charge of "cleaning his apartment" which had become code in the AIDS years for purging a person's porn, sex toys, drugs, etc. before family arrived.

Three months after receiving his degree, BL and Jeff returned to Tokyo. Given the limited opportunities for performing, some were surprised he returned. However, BL had a back-up plan as a means of artistic expression. After his return to Japan, BL became a recognized and popular figure at art exhibitions. By 1990, he had a one-man show of his paintings at Tokyo's Earth Art Gallery, and frequently showed his work in various shops and in the lobbies of several office buildings and residential towers.

BL's aesthetic is apparent in his paintings. He worked only in color and prided himself on never owning a tube of black paint. He displayed several of his pieces in his home with Jeff. BL was also fond of buying art. As a result, every inch of wall space and every surface in their flat was utilized for the display of paintings, statues, or sculpture. Their apartment was filled with so many beautiful and interesting things that guests wrestled with where to look.

Jeff and Bob had a cozy life together. Throughout their relationship, Jeff always did the cooking. BL liked doing laundry, especially hand laundry. He felt that certain items should be washed only by hand. Since moving to Japan, BL had grown increasingly careful about keeping his clothes in impeccable shape.

Though he wasn't necessarily superstitious, BL did follow the zodiac. He religiously read his Taurus horoscope for guidance, primarily in regards to fashion. He selected his clothing to match the lucky color of the day for his sign. But even his lucky color was no help on a rainy day. BL feared the sound of rain. Not storms. Not thunder, but rain. The sound of raindrops made him want to be held. He felt that if he was held closely and tightly enough, the rain couldn't touch him.

Never Can Say Goodbye

In 1993 BL returned to Chicago and stayed until 1998. This time Jeff stayed behind in Tokyo. Despite their long-distance relationship, the couple remained committed to one another and alternated annual one-month visits. The separations were difficult, but they made it work.

Jeff and BL shared a similar sentimental streak. They had pet names for one another, each calling the other Bunny. These terms of endearment were given an added dimension when BL happened upon two Bunny figurines in a resale shop. Each figure wore a little red suit; one was playing the tuba, the other the clarinet. In high school, Jeff had played the tuba and BL had played the clarinet. As a way to make their time apart more bearable, BL brought Bunny Tuba to Chicago while Jeff kept Bunny Clarinet in Tokyo. When BL and Jeff were reunited for their month-long visits, the visiting partner would pack Bunny Tuba or Bunny Clarinet and the figurines were placed side by side for the duration of the stay.

During this five-year stretch, Bob lived in a first floor apartment at 2156 W. Pierce Avenue in Wicker Park and attended University of Illinois-Chicago and then Northeastern University in graduate-level linguistics studies. By this time in his life, BL wasn't as studious as he had once been or maybe he didn't have the passion for linguistics that he'd had for Art History. He passed his classes, but he didn't shine as he had with his undergraduate degree.

During this time BL was also teaching at Truman College. He was often seen about town in one of his vintage shirts that featured exotic patterns and vibrant colors. Clothes and presentation remained a central part of BL's persona. When choosing his outfit and accessorizing, he rarely wore something that wouldn't get him noticed. Being seen was important. As BL often said, "Fashion is in the streets!"

Jewelry remained an obsession, too. BL always wanted more. At a jewelry store, or two, it was not unusual for him to have as many as five different items on layaway. Every week he made the pilgrimage to this or that store and paid another $5 dollars towards each piece. The process took a while, but eventually the baubles were his.

In 1995 BL met Lon, a fellow student he took under his wing. Lon had no idea about BL's celebrity and was surprised to see his new friend so widely recognized around town; in the grocery store, in restaurants, at galleries, on the bus, in the street, at museums, at a suburban mall, and of course, at the clubs. When BL arrived at an event at Vortex on North Halsted, the bar promoters were star struck. BL was a nightlife legend. A promoter asked him if he wanted to dance on stage. Rather than reply, BL simply smiled, extended a hand, and was led to the platform.

Leather bars were still among BL's favorite places. He was fond of calling himself the Hostess of the Leather Community. In those years he frequented AA Meat Market, Manhole, and Touché, which he pronounced as "Touchy." One night BL was at the Chicago Eagle when a fan from the Bistro days approached and said he had always loved his act as the Bearded Lady. BL asked the admirer how he knew he was the Bearded Lady. The befuddled patron said he thought he recognized him, but that the flowerpot earrings were the real giveaway.

Fans of BL were routinely surprised to encounter him around town. Since he had moved to another continent in the midst of the epidemic, many thought he had died. BL looked robust, almost unchanged from his early Bistro years. His energy was good and his heft appeared about the same. He'd always been a bit more than husky. His biggest concession to vanity was dyeing his hair.

After he began to gray, his mother, Kay, was adamant: she would not allow herself to be seen with a gray-haired son and made it emphatically clear he needed to do something about it. In retaliation, BL bought the reddest shade of Miss Clairol he could find and used it on his hair. Instead of being upset, Kay was overjoyed that her son had followed her wishes. He turned a lot of heads during their dinner, but she didn't mind. Kay did not object to standing out. She shared that trait with her son.

Don't Leave Me This Way

In 1998, BL returned to Tokyo. Before leaving Chicago he had an enormous amount of items (clothing, books, jewelry, etc.) shipped back to Japan. To accommodate his increasing number of belongings, Jeff had to rent the apartment next door. The couple now needed a minimum of five rooms instead of three.

In Tokyo, BL resumed teaching English as a Second Language despite never completing his Masters Degree. He taught high school, but also worked with slightly older students, mainly 18 and 19 year-olds, at a vocational school. When he was in front of a class, BL dressed accordingly. He took great pains to look professional, especially if he knew that pictures were being taken.

Following his return, BL began to contribute art columns in the English language press of Japan. He also continued to shop. To bolster his income, which allowed him to shop even more, BL started moonlighting at a place called Telephone English. The service allowed people to call in and practice their English skills over the telephone. Mostly this entailed listening and if the callers happened to get connected to BL, they got more than their money's worth. He could chat endlessly about topics from art to fashion, and from horticulture to film, to the everyday goings-on in his life. He quickly became the most requested talker by Telephone English callers.

BL also tutored several wealthy Japanese women who enjoyed having him over for tea to converse because his visits were a great help with their English skills. He intrigued the women. They had never met anyone like him, and doubted they ever would again.

By then BL was a successful and in-demand instructor. He was entertaining in the classroom and did his best to make learning interesting and fun. He taught ESL at several places, including the Language Instructors Guild, the Saitama YMCA, Sundai Travel College, Asuka and Arakawa High Schools, and Berlitz Language School.

In addition to choosing his own outfits for various jobs and engagements, BL also chose Jeff's clothes. As an unwritten household rule, Jeff was more or less forbidden to open closets. BL feared Jeff would discover the true size and extent of the Theiss-Bruce wardrobe. Because he didn't want to have to get rid of anything, every day he laid out Jeff's outfit.

For years BL's look, with his long hair and a very long beard, made him resemble a biker or a member of Z.Z. Top. When he eventually cut his long hair and stopped dyeing it, the change was dramatic. Japanese children began calling him Santa-san or Santa Claus. The nickname was for his looks as well as for his jolly demeanor. Santa-san was a role BL embraced wholeheartedly.

Art collector was another role BL adopted completely. With his passion for Asian Art at a peak, he began collecting pieces in earnest; primarily focusing on Chinese ceramics and Indian bronzes. He continued to buy until the Jeff Bruce-Bob Theiss collection grew to over 500 pieces. The items were primarily attained through annual trips to Shanghai and the surrounding area. On those sojourns to China, when the people saw his wild gray hair, they started calling him Karl Marx.

The Marx nickname was for his looks, but certainly not his beliefs. BL was an unapologetic, free-market capitalist. During most of his adult life, he identified as politically conservative on all but LGBT issues. His traditionalist stance on most matters was derived from his years of military service as well as his conservative upbringing. He shared many of the same views as his biological family. Sometimes he needed that connection.

As the Millennium drew to a close, BL was diagnosed with a rare blood cancer. The National Cancer Institute describes agnogenic myeloid metaplasia as, "a progressive, chronic disease in which the bone marrow is replaced by fibrous tissue and blood is made in organs such as the liver and the spleen, instead of in the bone marrow. This disease is marked by an enlarged spleen and progressive anemia." Both his father and grandfather had succumbed to blood cancers. At the time BL was given the diagnosis, the doctor told him he had a life expectancy of 2-20 years.

In 2001, his condition worsened. To survive, he required frequent transfusions and steroids to force his pancreas to produce blood. BL tried to have a good attitude and remain cheerful and inspiring. He was forever trying to get a smile from the doctors, the nursing staff, and everyone on the payroll. Before his first transfusion, the nurse read his name and blood type, "Bob Theiss, B+ [B positive]." Without missing a beat, BL answered, "I'll do my best, thanks."

The cold of winter somewhat helped alleviate the effects of his illness, but when the summer's heat arrived, his condition worsened. Sick as he was, BL never cried. He believed that crying changed nothing and only depleted his energy.

For his birthday in 2003, Jeff bought BL his first cellphone and a matching one for himself. In less than a month, BL was admitted to Tokyo Women's University Hospital. During his stay, Jeff used the birthday cellphone constantly, talking to BL, calling the nurses, notifying friends and family with updates on his illness. Both men were grateful for the technology. Cellphones helped connect them at a time that could have been even more isolating.

Despite his illness, BL was still a ruling queen and would "hold court" for those who visited his room on the 11th floor. He remained sassy. When a recently published author showed up at his bedside, BL demanded a signed copy of the book before promptly falling asleep.

In the end, in spite of his passion for collecting clothing, jewelry, and art, BL didn't care about *things* anymore; just people, just that Jeff and his friends and family were there. He was aware of what was happening and of the grave nature of his illness, but he also knew there was nothing he could do about it. He became resigned to the inevitable. BL was at peace with himself.

During his hospital stay, BL sometimes talked in his sleep. In those times he was heard to say things like, "Here we are in the south of France" and "Oh, this is most elegant." Mostly, during those final days, he just wanted Jeff to hold his hand. Touch was such a comfort. His final words were, "I love..."

He died during the third summer of his illness, on June 18, 2003. BL often professed that he wanted to live to be 100. He died at age 56. The cancer was more aggressive than the physicians expected. The official cause on his death certificate was listed as sepsis, caused by Myelofibrosis.

BL's body was cremated. Three days later, Jeff hosted a funeral service in their home. Coworkers, friends, family, and students overflowed the interior. Oddly reminiscent of his days at the Bistro, the line of people assembled to honor him one last time snaked down the block. They came to pay their respects and light a stick of incense before his ashes. It was said that the smoke could be seen over a block away.

At BL's request, Missoni handkerchiefs were distributed to the mourners so they might grieve in style. To combat the heat, those in attendance were given hand fans. As a result, each of the eighty-three mourners in the cramped quarters were cooling themselves with a hand fan, looking like a large gathering of butterflies, fluttering before BL's ashes. The visual seemed a fitting send-off.

There But for the Grace of God Go I

A small amount of BL's ashes were cast from First Bridge in Nanjing, China into the Yangtze River. The remaining ashes were eventually inurned in the Columbarium Wall at Chicago's Graceland Cemetery. As the urn was being placed in the wall, BL's friend Lon sang Handel's *Where'er You Walk*.

In addition to Jeff, BL was survived by his mother and sister as well as assorted relatives and numerous friends. By then many of his fans were dead, had forgotten him, or thought he had died years before. In the years of the AIDS pandemic those sorts of assumptions were common. Many people of a certain age stopped asking about those they hadn't seen in awhile. *Didn't you hear* had become too dreaded and too routine of a response.

Memorial contributions in BL's name were made to the Leukemia Society of America.

BL left behind a great deal. Some things he hoarded, like clothes. Other things he accumulated, like CDs. His music collection was primarily New Age and Classical with little of the Disco that had made him famous. He collected books. Indeed, Jeff sold upwards of 1,500 books after his death. The subject matter was predominantly Asian Art, but BL also collected first editions. He had an enormous inventory of accessories like jewelry and belts and dozens of hats. He also had dozens of shoes. When BL found a style of shoe he liked, he might buy it in every color. Many of his shoes were never worn.

BL was a collector of art. The Theiss/Bruce collection of artifacts primarily consisted of Chinese and Japanese ceramics and pottery. He also collected bronze Buddhist and Hindu figurines from China, India, and SE Asia. BL was meticulous in chronicling the details of each item he acquired, the date purchased, price, etc. into an extensive catalogue. Upon his death, he wanted all his art pieces to go to a museum. But the pieces in his collection, though varied and impressive, were not considered to be of museum quality. Jeff spent years selling some items, and giving others away. He tried to give some sort of memento to everyone who had known BL.

Some thought BL planned to open an upscale boutique someday. Friends found it easy to imagine him serving tea as shoppers admired his eclectic merchandise. Boutique owner seemed a perfect career for him because BL was thrilled to discuss anything and everything he had accumulated. He found it exciting to meet other collectors or people who appreciated such things. Indeed, BL could have stocked a shop several times over.

Jeff held several sales to liquidate many of BL's belongings. One sale featured nothing more than BL's extensive collection of Missoni items: scarves, gloves, sweaters, hats, and even rugs. Jeff felt it necessary to tell the staff at the main Missoni store in Tokyo that their most loyal foreign customer was gone. The clerk on duty said everyone knew him, and that all would be told.

Although BL was in many respects a hoarder, in the end he didn't keep much from his days in Chicago. Most of the items were sentimental: a keychain from the Bistro, some Al Carter Polaroid photos with friends and fans, and a binder of publicity photos and newspaper clippings. BL's biggest keepsake from his time in Chicago was the magnificent life-sized bronze made of his head in the mid-'80s.

BL was many things in his life and many things to many people. As in his iconic performances, BL was comprised of layer after layer after layer. He was a court jester, a crazed genius, and a force of nature. He exuded the gay community's unbridled joy, and captured the absurdity, electricity, and strange beauty of an era.

BL was beyond proper pronoun usage. He did genderfuck before genderfuck was a thing. He was a pioneering radical faerie working as a go-go boy in a gay urban jungle. He was an art collector, an artist, and most importantly, a work of art. BL was his own creation. He was persona as performance.

BL's enduring message was don't worry about being modest, being appropriate, or being over the top. He was all about celebrating beauty and the ecstasy of the moment. He saw us all in a constant state of changing and becoming.

    Move. Shed. Turn. Transform.

Bob Theiss' Final Days
(From the Journals of Jeffrey Mark Bruce)

Late May—A sore throat starts. Bob starts to eat less, not finishing some foods and deciding others aren't appealing.

June 5, Thursday—Bob goes to Tokyo Women's Hospital for a regular checkup and the doctors identify sepsis. I go to Aoyama Gakuin and then to my Ernst & Young student, Mr. Takiguchi, for the first time (normally on Wednesday). In the evening, we have a big fight. Bob is upset about food for his lunches and pushes me to get the recycling out of 101 because of his private student coming there for the first time on Sunday. I lose my temper and smash a glass on the floor as we argue back and forth. Also, I vow there won't be any recycling anymore. Later, I clean up the broken glass and we watch TV together. Around this time, Bob had a fever sleeping in our bed at night and decided the air conditioner on the new side would be better for him. I made him a bed of our three cushions covered with a sheet. Sometimes, I slept on the new side. Later, I slept next to him every night, as he might need something in the night.

June 7, Saturday—Bob worked a full day at Berlitz, but it wore him out. I met him at a station and we rode to the station down the street for Stiletto. Bob's hands were visibly shaking when he put on the jewelry he'd brought with him. It was hard for him to walk to the restaurant. Bob couldn't eat much, but talked a lot. He wasn't following what the waiter said very clearly and misunderstood him to have lived in Chicago, instead of Toronto. He tried to get him to say he'd been to the Bistro, so he could tell him who he was. At one point, he told Jim to take me out to clubs when he's gone. After dinner with Jim, we went home by taxi because Bob was simply too weak. The Taxi had global positioning which was the first time I'd seen it in a cab. We went along streets that were interesting to see and it rained some.

June 8, Sunday—In the morning, Bob taught his student at home for the first and only time. He was worried about the student stepping on glass from the incident on Thursday. Actually, I stepped on the only glass, except for an ambulance worker on Sunday. After his student, Bob rested. Later, we met Vivien and Dan at the Hilton in Shinjuka to go to a nearby Lebanese restaurant they knew well. Bob tried to eat, but had great difficulty. It was virtually the last time he tried to eat solid food. However, he followed the conversation much better than the night before and there was lots of laughing all around. Afterwards, we again went home by taxi because of how weak Bob had become.

June 10, Tuesday—I worked at Sekisui as usual and Bob worked at Berlitz. Like so many times before, we meet after work at Kanamecho Station. Even when he was stronger, meeting allowed us a few extra minutes as we walked together and let Bob get rid of his bag, either for me to carry or to put in my bicycle basket. That night, we had to stop frequently, including long stops at the Family Mart for a beverage and at the Laundromat on the small lane for a rest.

June 11, Wednesday—Bob showered before going to work, but was too weak to pay attention to how he looked. I had to comb his hair for him on the street as we walked to the bus stop. By this point, walking to the station was too much. Luckily, he had a class at Asuka in which he could normally sit down. After teaching two hours, I walked him to the station but it took us an hour to get there with stops in the lobby of the school and along the way on a little lane. Still, his mood wasn't bad. I put him on a bus at Ikebukuro. It wasn't the one with the closest stop to our home but he was able to get off and walk home. That evening, he should've worked at ALE but another worker wanted to trade, so he took the evening later in the month when Matt was expected from America.

June 12, Thursday—Bob went to Tokyo Women's Hospital for a regular checkup. He was advised to enter the hospital, but refused. He didn't tell me he had done that, however. I went to Aoyama Gakuin and came home expecting to find a message that Bob had entered Tokyo Women's Hospital since he was clearly sicker than before his birthday when he was first admitted. Bob came dragging in slowly. He was supposed to teach at Third Commercial High School, but didn't go and didn't call. He said he would call the next day. We watched a taped "ER," our last television together. Thankfully, the episode wasn't the one in which Bob's favorite character, Mark, discovered he was dying of reoccurring brain cancer. I saw that episode as the first one after Bob was gone. If he'd seen it when terribly ill it would've made Bob feel worse.

June 13, Friday—Bob had put off renewing his alien registration card to almost the last day, so we took a taxi to the ward office. At the entrance, he saw wheelchairs and wanted one, but I thought it might make a bad impression at the time he turned in the application. We'd forgotten to bring photos, so I had to take him out to a photo booth. I ran off looking for the booth, but had to have the directions explained again. Once I found it, I slowly walked him there with him holding onto me going and coming back. This would be Bob's last photo. Once he was ready to apply, I had to help him down into a chair and up again afterward. I had to run off to the bank while he waited for his papers to be processed. Normally, he should've had to come to the counter when his number was called. They realized how weak Bob was and the worker came and sat next to him, a startling variation from official procedure in Japan. Afterward, we took the elevator up to the health insurance counter where I spoke for Bob while he sat and rested. Then, I put him into a taxi for home and went off to Aoyama Gakuin. At home, Bob called Carol for the last time. That night, we slept together on the new side, but Bob was already becoming disoriented. He would wake up in the middle of the night and think morning had come.

June 14, Saturday—Bob was too weak to shower before work, but took some liquids. I put him into a taxi to Nerima Berlitz and went to work at Nullarbor. After a while at Nullarbor, a call came from Bob that they'd sent him home sick and he needed me to come home to make lunch for him, which of course would be liquids. Later that evening, he tried to eat solid food chopped very fine, but couldn't keep it down. Most of the time he slept well. At one point, I was on the old side on the computer when he needed me and he wound up wetting himself. During the night, he would do it a couple more times. Much later on, he was sitting in his chair on the old side and said he needed to go to the bathroom, but didn't have the strength to get up. Finally, he got to the bathroom and then to our bed. I knew he was bad off and sent an email to Dr. Mizoguchi. Still, Bob was talking about sticking with the plan of resting at home until his hospital appointment on Monday. I knew neither Bob nor I could make it through Sunday with nothing more than rest at home.

June 15, Sunday—Around sunrise, Bob says he was scared and I took that as approval to call for an ambulance. Several technicians gave Bob a checkup on the bed and then helped him to the ambulance, loading him onto an upright wheelchair. He was unable to walk on his own. One of the technicians stepped on a piece of broken glass from my blowup on June 5 and complained to his coworker about that. One elderly neighbor saw him leaving and bowed low to the ambulance as he was loaded in. Bob went to Tokyo Women's Hospital with the siren blasting in the light morning traffic. I was sitting next to him answering questions in Japanese and sometimes crying. At the emergency room, various tests were done and I answered a lengthy set of questions from an English-speaking attending female doctor. At one point, an ultrasound monitor was used to find the reason for his clearly distended abdomen. Bob joked and said, "I know for a fact, I'm not pregnant." Later he demanded to be taken to his room. The doctors thought he was talking about going home, but he meant the room he'd had when he was in a few days before his birthday. When taken to the large room up on the 11th floor, it took some time to convince Bob that this would be his room. Around noon, I went home for a few hours and sent emails and made calls about Bob. Around 3:00 p.m., I went back to the hospital for a few hours. Jim Leone came as Bob's first visitor. Already, Bob was sleeping a lot. Also, he was carefully getting the most communication out of every word he said. When one doctor said he'd spoken to "Sensei" (Dr. Mozoguchi). Bob's only answer was, "And?" I had to explain his question as the attending doctor failed to realize that was a complete question in a single word. Around 6:00 p.m., I left again. Shortly after I got home, the hospital called to say Bob's condition had suddenly worsened and I should come back. I dashed out and got a taxi. The driver saw I was upset and rushed me as quickly as conditions allowed. Bob stabilized, so around 3:00 a.m. I went home again. Late at night, I sent out faxes to Bob's and my employers explaining the situation.

June 16, Monday—I returned to the hospital around 10:00 a.m. By that time, I'd missed work at Asuka and then my fax was found. Barry came as Bob's first visitor of the day, followed by Greg and Kathy. Bob was pretty lively talking with Greg giving him a hard time asking where his copy of Greg's book about a Canadian artist was located. Greg offered to get a library copy for him and Bob loudly protested he didn't want a library copy. When visitors weren't in the room, Bob would fall into a sleep with vivid dreams. He spoke a lot with phrases from his dreams, "Now, everyone introduce yourself." (a teaching dream). "Here we are in the middle of France," (a traveling dream) and some phrases I couldn't interpret ("One thing I've noticed is..."). Sometimes when he was awake we could carry on a conversation. I asked him about a Do Not Resuscitate order, but he refused. He said, "New things are being discovered every day." It pained me to think he thought my intention was to keep him from being troublesome. He was able to remember what we'd said and told some visitors about our disagreement. When I told him Cynthia would agree to the order he said clearly in one dream, "Cynthia, would you do that to Mother?" Donald Fountain and Kara Besher visited and Kara brought holy water from Tibet. Three Berlitz workers came, Mochizuki-sensi came from Asuka HS and Greg Irwin and his lover, Ken, came. Two ALR workers came, Brent, the Gotos who make outfits for Donald, Kato-sensei and also Vice Principal Kobayashi came from Asuka HS. At one point, someone observed that it was like a gathering of the old queens of Tokyo since several of us go back many, many years. In all, 18 visitors came.

June 17, Tuesday—Immediately, Bob greets me with an accusation that I was having an affair. Apparently, he woke up in the night and noticed I wasn't there. I laughed about it but wondered what I could do it get him to understand that I would go home and sleep at night. Anthony from ALE came and I thought Bob was confused when he called him Johnny, but later I found that Anthony went by the nickname. Daisuke and his brother Jun arrived, but Bob slept most of the time. Ana brought him flowers and when Donald and Hideo came in, Bob reacted clearly to Hideo being there. Hideo had missed several parties for one reason or another and Bob noted that he was there with, "Oh, my god!" Also, Bob asked about Donald's father before he left as Donald's father was also very ill at the time. Donald would be leaving for America to be at his father's bedside the next day. Arakita and Kitada-sensei arrived and then more ALE workers. The ALE workers tried to raise Bob's spirits with chocolates and implored Bob to recover. At the end of the workday, Kathy Callaghan came. Bob was momentarily alert enough to pump her for information about where she was currently teaching as he had done for many years. He often drifted off, but would let her kiss him. Finally, a Japanese teacher from Asuka came and stayed a long time praying and singing. I felt it was nice that she made such a big effort. Since I knew Bob was dying, I also thought hearing hymns and prayers around him might rekindle his early Christian upbringing. Finally, the Japanese teacher left and then Kathy went. After awhile I told Bob it was time for him to rest again and he said, "OK," and it was time for me to go home and rest and he said, "OK," again. That night, he seemed clear with what was happening.

June 18, Wednesday—I heard the rooster at Takamatsu Elementary and immediately thought I'd better get up and go to the hospital. I arrived around 8:00 a.m. and found Bob in a terrible state. He was moaning and calling out in a voiceless sound like an infant. He was also twitching as well as shifting around on the bed like he couldn't get comfortable. A nurse asked what I wanted them to do. When they explained his sounds where vocalizations and didn't mean he was in pain, I said they didn't need to sedate him more to make him stop. I knew Japanese relatives would likely be shocked by infantile behavior and want their loved one to be drugged until they looked peaceful. I wanted Bob to have a chance to communicate or at least understand me as long as he wasn't in pain. In fact, I could speak to him and it would calm him down. I told him the rooster had told me, "Go to Bobby," and that calmed him down. While I was sitting with him, he often put his hand down to his underwear. I was afraid he'd pull his catheter out, but he didn't do that. Sometimes, his movements still seemed quite thoughtful when he'd put his hands together as if in prayer or cross his legs or arms. During the morning, he managed to say five words. First, he said, "Carol," so I called her from his bedside telephone. She could talk to him, but he couldn't talk anymore. Next, I read Thomas Hickey's email in which he spoke of Bob going to heaven to paint and photograph the angels, especially the buff ones. When I said angels, Bob said, "Little angels," so I called him my Little Angel for the last hours of his life and told him to go to heaven. Then, the phone rang. Cynthia in America got the telephone switchboard number off the Internet and called. Bob became very agitated and struggled to say, "I love you, Cynthia," but only managed, "I love..." his last two words. Around 10:45AM Dr. Okamura asked me to step to the meeting room to discuss what to do when Bob's heart stops. The very moment we sat down, nurses rushed in and we had to run back. Bob's heart had stopped, but efforts to revive him were quickly seen to be ineffective. Death was pronounced at 10:54AM. Soon, nurses began to prepare the body and I helped, taking off Bob's grandfather's ring. At 11:30AM, Vivien Cohen arrived to visit. Later, Kamiya-sensei also arrived. Later, Vivien took me home to get trousers and a shirt for Bob. I returned and helped the nurses dress Bob in green pants, a Missoni tee shirt and a Jhane Barnes shirt. The nurses had by then washed Bob's hair and clipped his fingernails. At one point, while everyone was out of the room, Ana walked in on her own and found Bob's body. Andrew and Hun also arrived. Vivien, Ana, Andrew and Jun went with me when Bob's body was taken down to a basement chapel. On the way down, the elevator stopped at every floor, giving patients unpleasant shocks when the door opened and they saw Bob's sheet-draped body. At the chapel, I agreed to leave so it could be set up for Buddhist ceremonies. The five of us each offered prayers: mine was a secular spoken statement, Ana's was silent, Vivien's was in Hebrew, Andrew's was silent and Jun's was in Japanese. When I went upstairs to clear out his room, Kawaguchi-san arrived. I took her down to chapel and then she helped me load all the flowers into a taxi in the rain and I went home. I rode to the Toshima ward office and applied at the basement after-hours office for permission to cremate Bob. When I got home, I called the hospital and they scheduled the cremation.

June 19, Thursday—It was a hot day and I dressed very informally for the cremation in blue jeans and a tee shirt. I took Aoyama Level I essays to correct as I had to get ready for the next week. At the hospital, I was accompanied by Kaori, an English-speaking nurse, to the chapel. Then, doctors and nurses of the hematology department came down in pairs and groups. I had a long wait while they prepared Bob for transport, loading him into his wooden coffin. Once he was ready, 12 people came again from the hematology department and we went through ceremonial Thank Yous. First, they lined up and bowed together to the hearse that held Bob in his coffin. Next, they bowed to me standing beside the coffin. Finally, I returned the bow. Each bow was very slow and low and meant much more than the quick bobs of heads you see daily, All was done at the hospital; I got in and rode off with Bob, the driver, and a worker from the chapel/morgue section who would guide me at the crematorium. When we arrived. Bob's coffin was immediately wheeled to an oven with his name on it. A very large Japanese family group was in the communal room and I felt a little sorry that I'd dressed informally. Soon, a large group, possibly from Southern Europe, arrived. I was given a chance to say a last good-bye through a special window in the top of the coffin. After that, Bob was loaded in and I was shown to the crematorium coffee shop. I sat there for about an hour correcting papers and drinking coffee. The hospital worker came to get me and I was shown back just as Bobo's remains came out of the oven. A crematorium worker shoveled his bones onto a large tray. The ashes, I later found, are vacuumed up and thrown away. I was directed to pick up chopsticks and use them to move the biggest bones from the tray to Bob's urn. The crematorium worker picked up the middle-sized bones with another pair of chopsticks and then dumped in the little bones. He had to pack it down some. Finally, he showed me a tooth and some skull pieces and arranged them on the top. He screwed on the lid, put it into a box, put a cover over it and then tied it with a furoshiki. The hospital worker confirmed that I planned to go home by train and that I knew the location of the station. Even though groups normally arrive and leave by car or taxi, I found it easy enough to carry the bundle. The box was still warm from the oven heat. I presumed people along the street would've known what I was carrying. By the time I was on the train or switching at Shinjuka Station, I was just a person with a bundle. When I got to Kanmecho Station, I followed a path Bob and I had walked together hundreds of times. As I walked, I quietly described what I saw, sights Bob would've known. Later, Jim and Hiro came by and we put in a busy evening cleaning out the apartment so it would be ready for the memorial service on Saturday.

June 20, Friday—I worked all day long by myself trying to get the apartments cleared out for the memorial service. The emphasis wasn't on emptying closets or getting rid of unnecessary things, just clearing out visible areas. I was so deep into the process that when Greg called and said he was with other teachers I wondered how they happened to be together. I'd entirely forgotten I was off from teaching at that point. That evening, Kami-sensei from Arakawa Commercial came by to pay his respects early and left flowers.

June 21, Saturday—There still was tons to do and Ana came by around noon to pitch in. When my energy was failing, she still seemed to be full of energy. After several busy hours, she went home to get cleaned up. I went out and got sushi for the guests. Yanese-sensei formerly of Asuka arrived and left before everyone else. Before the actual time of the memorial service, a stream of people started arriving and were offering prayers and burning incense in front of Bob's remains. Soon there was such a crowd that the front door had to be left open and the apartment didn't have a chance to cool off. People were milling outside or leaving once they'd offered their prayers. At some point, people who didn't quite know the way could simply follow the crowd coming from Senkawa Station. Throughout the prayers, I took up my spot at the corner of the room bowing to each person as they bowed to me. For quite awhile, Akaida-san sat next to me. I showed everyone the various pictures I'd gathered of Bob at various points in his life including a big one with Cynthia in their childhood and one of him looking down in a pensive expression. Especially, I showed the Yamato children and Mrs. Yamato the one of Bob dressed as Santa Claus. The incense almost became overwhelming, so I asked Kara and Kathy to pass out hand fans. Fumiko especially had trouble and had to leave quickly. Once most of the people had left, I could get up and walk around. Since many of the foreigners had brought food, they stuck around. I made sure everyone had a drink and a fan and read the statements I'd prepared, Bob's eulogy and the story of his grandfather's ring. Eventually, it dwindled down to Ana, Kathy, Chris and a couple other people. At last, I was alone.

Eulogy for Robert Theiss, Read at Memorial Service in the two-room apartment on June 21, 2003

Bob lived to be 56, but he had a full life. He taught in Japan for 12 years at Language Instructors Guild, the Saitama YMCA, Sundai Travel College, Asuka and Arakawa High Schools, Berlitz Language School, Telephone English, and many other places. He enjoyed visiting museums in his free time. He painted and he collected ceramics as well as bronze Buddhas and other figures. He always loved parties and he loved to talk. When his hair started to turn gray, children began to call him Santa-san. Like Santa Claus, Bob had a jolly personality. But talking was not the only thing that Bob was good at. He listened well, too. He knew that every student had a good and interesting story to tell. He worked hard to bring that story to life. He may not be with us anymore but as you go out into the world and tell your story, remember Bob. Then, he is alive and you are too through the stories you tell.

My First Gay Bar
By Richard Knight, Jr.

In the late spring of 1976 I was 18 and was going to the College of DuPage, the junior college in Glen Ellyn, Illinois. Marla was my best friend and we were both heavily involved in the theater department. I was gay but out only to Marla, who was all knowing and all accepting. We met Patti after seeing her perform in a one-act play. Offstage she was tough and wickedly funny and a kindred spirit. She was married to Jack and after meeting him we realized that Jack was gay and further, that Patti was fine with it. They obviously had what was then a relatively new kind of relationship – an open marriage. They were the hippest people I had ever met and they fascinated me. Not long after meeting them they invited us to go with them to their favorite place – the Bistro nightclub, the renowned gay Chicago nightspot.

I had never been in a gay bar and wasn't sure exactly what they were. Only a year earlier I had moved to the Chicago suburbs from a tiny town in western Nebraska where such places didn't seem to exist. We accepted Patti and Jack's invitation – me, with a combination of nerves and youthful bravado, Marla with a practiced shrug of her shoulders – and drove down to the city with them which was thrilling for me in and of itself. At the door, I anxiously offered a phony gun license as my ID – Marla had expertly put it together using the photo I provided – and it worked. They gave Marla a bit of a hard time but when Patti and Jack protested – they were regulars – the doorman let her in.

I could hear the music throbbing even before I walked through the darkened entryway and into the blaze of lights in the first room. There was a large circular bar to the right with banquettes scattered about. Dancing on the bar was an androgynous, David Bowie look alike with platinum blonde hair. His skin was pale as a ghost and he was shirtless and thin. He exuded bored self-confidence. I couldn't take my eyes off him. "You Should Be Dancing" by the Bee Gees – which I'd never heard – was just finishing and the next song (which I later found out was "Try Me, I Know We Can Make It" by Donna Summer) was starting up. The banquettes weren't packed but there were enough head turning people in the room that I knew I had left Kansas far behind.

A wide staircase led up to the darkened dance floor. Patti and Jack had given Marla and me a moment to take in the atmosphere but now they wanted the action of the dance floor. They turned and grabbed our hands and pulled us into the packed room and we literally plunged into a disco inferno. With wild abandon, both Patti and Jack began dancing frenetically, caught up in the pulsating music and the sensual energy of the people packed on the floor. I gazed around the room, catching glimpses of the glittering faces between the shafts of light from the neon strobes and the swirling mirror balls overhead. I'd never seen people like this. The hair; the make-up; the nonchalance; the lust for life – it was all outside my limited imagination.

I was terrified and thrilled at the same time. The DJ went into the next song, "Honey Bee" by Gloria Gaynor. Then, behind me, the energy level ramped up even higher and the crowd surged toward me. I turned around and realized that it was the larger than life emanation on the tiny elevated stage next to me that was the focus of everyone's attention. I looked up at the figure perched there, high above the crowd. She was wearing a floor length, gold Lamé gown topped with a wide brimmed gold Lamé beekeeper's hat and veil. She held a large, matching gold Lamé hand mirror in one hand, completely covering her face as she danced on the stage. The effect was dazzling. As the song reached a crescendo, she triumphantly yanked the mirror away and revealed her face as she lip-synced to the song. She was heavily bearded and exuberant and at the moment of her unmasking the crowd – if possible – went even crazier. I glanced over at Patti who was laughing, delighted at my fascinated, shocked reaction. Part of me thought I'd entered the fifth circle of Hell but the other part intrinsically knew that I was witnessing a life changing moment.

I was right. Life was never the same after that first delirious glimpse of the legendary Bearded Lady ramping up the crowd higher and higher that initial night at the Bistro. Her delight in performing infected everyone and was the highlight of my first visit to a gay bar. I saw her many times after that – Patti and Jack took Marla and I to the Bistro often (including New Year's Eve of 1976) – but nothing ever came close to topping that first encounter.

In lieu of an Index, here is a quote by BL himself:

"THE ONLY TIME A GAY PERSON GOES STRAIGHT IS WHEN THEY GO STRAIGHT TO THE INDEX TO CHECK THE NAMES."

This book would not have been possible without help on numerous fronts. Enormous thanks to all who truly helped to make this a community effort:

Darr Gapshis, Tommy [TL] Noble, Carol Cheeseman, Ron Veltman, Richard Knight, Jr., Ron Ehemann, Daniel Goss, Peter Bellinder, Jimmy Blythe, Donald Fountaine, the staff of Gerber Hart Library and Archives, Victor Salvo, The Legacy Project, Richard Dahlman, Jimmy D'Ambrosia, James Scalfani, Chris C. Stray, Wil Brant, Chuck Shotwell, Lon Ellenberger, Billy Miller, Jeff Berry, Kim Christian Olson, Don Eric, Dan Bell, John Koch, Paul Mikos, Daniel Dever, Zander Mander, Rick Karlin, Max Bailey, Shane Khosropour, Michael Kutza, Ronald "Dodger" Chupich, Tom Palazzolo, Sukie de la Croix, Ed Egan, Paul Escriva, Dan Neniskis, Marge Summit, Grant Smith, Gerald Pagorek, Gary Chichester, Marc Hauser, Jaime Krohn, Richard Cooke, Rob Colucci, Lori Cannon, Dean Ogren, David Plambeck, Pat Cummings, Tracy Baim, Andrew Davis, Carrie Maxwell, several anonymous interviewees, Scott Free and Homolatte, the Chicago Prime Timers, the Facebook page members of Dugan's Bistro The Ultra Disco, the Facebook page members of Paradise Chicago - Boystown 1980s.

Thank you to Windy City Times, GayLife, and Gay Chicago Magazine.

Thanks to Andie McKenzie Meadows for the awesome author photo and Kirk Williamson for the cover design and putting it all together.

Thank you to my husband, Carl Blando, for his continued love and patience.

And lastly, a big thanks to Jeffrey Mark Bruce, without whose generous cooperation and assistance none of this would have been possible.

Writer and grassroots historian **Owen Keehnen** is the author of several books of fiction including the gay novels The Sand Bar, Love Underground, and Young Digby Swank; the horror novel Doorway Unto Darkness; and the Lambda Literary Award nominated collection Night Visitors. His fiction, essays, and interviews have appeared in dozens of periodicals nationwide. He authored the reference book The LGBT Book of Days and over 100 of his interviews with various LGBT authors and activists were collected in the book We're Here, We're Queer. With Tracy Baim he coauthored the historical biographies; Leatherman: The Legend of Chuck Renslow, Jim Flint: The Boy from Peoria, and Vernita Gray: From Woodstock to The White House. Keehnen is the cofounder and senior biographer of the LGBT organization, The Legacy Project that seeks to bring proper recognition to LGBT people and their contributions throughout history. He co-edited Nothing Personal: Chronicles of Chicago's LGBTQ Community 1977-1997 and wrote ten of the biographical essays in the LGBT history book Out and Proud in Chicago. He is the author of the Starz collections, a four volume series of interviews with gay porn stars. He's had monologues adapted for the stage, edited the Windy City Times Pride Literary Supplement, and cofounded the horror film website racksandrazors.com. He lives in Chicago with his husband Carl and their dogs. He was inducted into the Chicago LGBT Hall of Fame in 2011.

Jeff Bruce is a university and high school instructor in Tokyo with numerous language teaching publications. He has made Japan his permanent home and has a Japanese partner of many years.

Richard Knight, Jr. is a writer, filmmaker and musician with a 30-year career in Chicago as a freelance creative. He is the founder and President of the Queer Film Society, a non-profit group devoted to promoting queer film in Chicago.

Also By Owen Keehnen
Night Visitors
Love Underground
The Matinee Idol
Young Digby Swank
Vernita Gray: From Woodstock to the White House
The LGBT Book of Days
Gay Press, Gay Power – contributor
The Sand Bar
We're Here, We're Queer
Jim Flint: The Boy From Peoria
Leatherman: The Legend of Chuck Renslow
Doorway Unto Darkness
Nothing Personal: Chronicles of Chicago's LGBTQ Community 1977-1997 – co-editor
Rising Starz
Ultimate Starz
Out and Proud in Chicago – contributor
More Starz
Starz

www.ingramcontent.com/pod-product-compliance
Lightning Source LLC
Chambersburg PA
CBHW070738020526
44118CB00035B/1493